SWEET CRAVINGS

sweet
CRAVINGS

50 Seductive Desserts
for a Gluten-Free Lifestyle

KYRA BUSSANICH

Photography by Leela Cyd

TEN SPEED PRESS
Berkeley

Contents

Cookies, Brownies, and Bar Treats
CHILDHOOD REVISITED

Puddings, Cakes, and Other Pastries
COMFORT AND AMAZE!

Award-Winning Cupcakes
LITTLE TREATS THAT PACK BIG TASTE

Tarts, Pies, and Puffs
DESSERTS TO IMPRESS

Preface

Looking back on my life, it seems obvious that I was destined to become a pastry chef.

Even when I was still too young to read, the heroine of my favorite book was a badger named Frances who loved to eat bread and jam.

When I was twelve, an age when most other girls were cutting out photos of teen idols from *YM* magazine, I was combing through my subscription to *Martha Stewart Living*, tearing out dessert recipes. By age fourteen, I was responsible for making dinner for my family two nights a week (Mondays spaghetti and Thursdays baked rice pudding with a gingersnap crust). I saved my allowance to buy cookbooks with full-color photos. I baked for slumber parties and family birthdays, and by the time I was sixteen, I was making all the holiday pies for family celebrations. In college, I used baking for stress reduction, handing out cookies and lemon bars to all grateful comers. I even used money intended for textbooks to instead buy my first KitchenAid mixer.

So why, then, did it take me so long to realize that baking was my calling? I'd always loved to bake, but it was something I did for fun, in my spare time: I didn't consider it a serious career. And then I went gluten-free.

When I first began my gluten-free journey eight years ago—having been diagnosed with an autoimmune condition that barred my eating goodies made with flour—I trudged through each stage of mourning for my comforting dessert staples: cinnamon rolls, scones, cakes, pies, tarts, and doughnuts. I combed through gluten-free cookbooks and websites for recipes to re-create my favorite treats, but, overwhelmingly, the message I kept getting was, "Lower your expectations: without flour and other 'critical ingredients,' a gluten-free cake will never have the same good flavor and texture as a 'regular' cake."

With that disheartening news, I glumly began trying to bake gluten-free. While there were several close approximations of the desserts I was trying to create, nothing impressed me as tasting like "the real thing."

Without a gluten-free go-to resource to advise me, I had to find my own way, beginning with attending Le Cordon Bleu's patisserie and baking program. This school changed my outlook. I could either perpetually feel I was missing out (and it's difficult to be a first-rate baker without taste-testing your creations)—or take positive action. I chose the latter. Armed with my newly gleaned information about the chemistry and function of ingredients, I'd come home after class and begin experimenting with gluten-free flours to see if I could re-create what I had made in class that day. Admittedly, in the beginning, I turned out a few hockey pucks. But as I kept experimenting, I gradually developed a trove of trusted recipes.

Once I had come up with a handful of cakes that were really good, I started sharing them with friends and family. My first cake offering was Persian Love Cake, now very popular in my bake shop. The combination of spicy cardamom and warm, toasty pistachios, topped

with cardamom Italian meringue buttercream, was a hit with everyone who tried it.

Shortly thereafter, I got a phone call from a gluten-free family friend who was getting married. I happily scheduled a cake tasting for the blissful couple. We met, they tasted the Persian Love Cake, Raspberry Beret (a vanilla cake topped with raspberry Italian meringue buttercream), and Lemon Cake, and chose all three for their wedding. Soon after the wedding, a guest in attendance called me and asked if I could make cupcakes for a baby shower. The calls escalated: I received several requests from guests at the baby shower—who weren't even gluten-free eaters!—who thought my cupcakes were delicious and wanted to know if I made birthday cakes. The only marketing I ever did was taking my cupcakes and other treats to parties and letting people sample, and business increased as word spread.

For the first eighteen months, I ran my bake shop as a custom-order business from my certified home kitchen, but that all changed one Tuesday evening. I have always loved watching the Food Network, and my husband and I were reclining in front of *Cupcake Wars* when he suggested I apply for the show. I had heard this before, from multiple people who told me they thought my cupcakes were the best they had ever eaten—gluten-free or not—and on this particular night, I agreed to try. I pulled out the laptop, sent off a quick email to the *Cupcake Wars* website, and pressed Send.

My phone rang a few hours later. Jessica, the show's casting director, was on the line and asked if I could submit a two-minute

video—the next day. This didn't give me much chance to think of a creative hook, but, none-theless, my husband pulled out his handheld camera and we filmed a short video (http://tiny.cc/KyraCCWAudition). I sent it off, deciding that the producers would either like it or not. Then I got nervous about the idea of competing head-to-head with other successful bakers on camera. What if the judges said—on camera—that my cupcakes were awful? Or worse, what if I succumbed to stage fright and messed up my recipes?

With these thoughts circling through my head, by the time the producer called to invite me on the show, I was a ball of nerves. But in the back of my mind was the hope that if I did compete, and the judges loved what I made, I could help change the false idea that gluten-free baked goods are either completely disgusting or just barely edible. I could help people see that gluten-free cakes can be just as delicious, if not more so, than gluten-full.

I felt like the underdog going in: I was the first gluten-free baker to appear on the show, and I was judged on whether these were excel-lent cupcakes, not on whether they were "good cupcakes for being gluten-free." To my relief, the judges' comments were extremely positive, and I wound up making it to the final round before being knocked out of the competition.

The following season, the producer asked if I'd like to compete in a redemption episode—this time against other bakers who also lost in the final round. Hoping I had learned some-thing from my first appearance and relishing the challenge, I agreed—and this time I won. The only mention of my cupcakes being completely gluten-free came in the last four seconds of the show: not once did I mention to the judges that I was baking gluten-free and competing against traditional bakers. I had won based simply on taste.

The next season, I again received a call from the producers. They were planning an all-star version of the show called *Cupcake Champions*, with sixteen previous winners competing for the Grand Championship. I said yes, won the semifinal show, and advanced to the Grand Finals in June 2012. Even though I was the runner-up overall, I felt like I had proven without a shadow of a doubt that gluten-free can compete against the "best of the best" of traditional baking.

Early on during the *Cupcake Wars* whirl-wind, I decided to open my very own brick-and-mortar bake shop. I am fortunate enough to live in a small suburban community (right outside Portland) that is extremely supportive of local businesses, and I knew I wanted to keep my shop local. After spending months scouring real estate listings, I stumbled on a charming brick building in the heart of down-town Lake Oswego. There were wide windows facing the street and twenty-foot ceilings, and, though the space was tiny, I had a vision for how it could be transformed into a warm, bright bakery.

After three months of tearing down walls, outfitting the shop with ovens and mixers, and fine-tuning my recipes, we opened the doors. Initially, I wasn't sure what to expect. After all, how many gluten-free people could there possibly be in our area? But the response has been overwhelming. We now sell more than a thousand freshly made cupcakes, cinnamon rolls, scones, cookies, doughnuts, rolls, bars, and ice cream sandwiches every day—all from 750 square feet of bake shop space. And all gluten-free.

Indeed, eating gluten-free, once seen as an oddity or only appropriate for a very few, has hit the mainstream. Awareness continues to rise about celiac disease and other auto-immune disorders (such as colitis, Crohn's disease, lupus, rheumatoid arthritis, and Hashimoto's) that can benefit from a gluten-free diet. Almost everybody knows at least one person who has recently started eating gluten-free. And then there are those who are gluten-free for other benefits, even without a diagnosed disorder.

Increasing awareness means that ready-made gluten-free foods on supermarket shelves are becoming more prevalent and better tasting. Five years ago, I had to make a trip to Whole Foods or another specialty foods store to buy gluten-free crackers. Today I can go to my local Safeway or Ralph's and find those same brands—and many more! However, there is no guarantee that every company can prevent cross-contamination with wheat or other allergens; and while buying ready-to-eat packaged foods off the shelf is certainly convenient, it can never compare to the best home recipes freshly made from scratch.

In *Sweet Cravings*, I provide proven recipes designed for you as a home cook to create gluten-free, delectable treats. Indeed, this cookbook will help you bake scrumptious desserts that your friends and family are unlikely to know are gluten-free (unless you tip them off in advance, or they see this book propped open on your counter). With these recipes, a single deliciously made dessert can be shared by a family or group of friends, and no one is left out, feels "different," or has to eat something "special." In fact, the desserts in this book are all special and — as numerous customers in my bake shop (as well as the *Cupcake Wars* judges) can attest—delightful to everyone.

With this book as your secret source, you can create irresistible cupcakes, buttery scones, and mouthwatering fruit tarts, instead of simply having to do without; don't miss the fun of blowing out candles on a birthday cake and being able to have a slice, or waking up to Christmas morning scones fresh out of the oven that taste even better than they smell. Everyone will love the taste and texture of these pastries *and* safely be able to eat them. What could be better?

Introduction

Superior Gluten-Free Baking

Are you like me—a "nourisher"? Someone who enjoys creating things that make a real difference in others' lives? Do you enjoy making people happy—through food—and coming up with something that at once elicits oohs and aahs and makes their day?

Well, this book is definitely for you. It's an opportunity to do all this—and much more.

When I appeared on the Food Network's *Cupcake Wars*, one of the judges—to my surprise and delight—called me the "inspirational 'It Girl' for gluten-free baking." And I'm bringing that inspiration to this book so that you, too, can wow your friends and family "judges." With these recipes as your guide, *you* can create light, fluffy cakes, buttery scones,

rich and impressive ice cream desserts, silky tiramisu, and more.

But, more importantly, this book is to help you discover that gluten-free baking can be tastier, better textured, and more appealing than traditional wheat-flour baking, and to make it easy for you to share your baking passion with those who eat gluten-free and still create addicting desserts for those who don't.

I think there's something magical about creating desserts that

- bring people together, so everyone can share the same special sweets

- are safe for your family and guests to eat, regardless of whether they have a

1

diagnosed gluten allergy, sensitivity, or intolerance

· taste even better than "regular," gluten desserts, meaning that you can indulge and still feel healthy afterward

And I'm going to share this magic with you.

The Scoop on Gluten

You may know that gluten—a protein in wheat and several other grains—means "glue" in Latin. It can play havoc with digestive and immune systems. Many people feel better or find that a range of symptoms disappear when they avoid gluten. For some, shunning gluten is a necessity and not a choice. For example, celiac disease is a genetic disorder that impairs the body's ability to properly absorb and process the gluten protein found in wheat, rye, barley, and other grains, and is treatable only by completely removing gluten from one's diet. The Celiac Disease Foundation reports that 1 in every 133 Americans has celiac disease, whether they know it or not. In addition, I've heard many nutritional therapists and naturopathic doctors strongly recommend that anyone with an inflammatory process or autoimmune disease—including Crohn's, fibromylagia, autism, ADHD, lupus, arthritis, and Hashimoto's—should avoid gluten, as it can trigger a negative immune response. According to the National Institutes of Health (NIH), autoimmunity is the underlying cause of more than a hundred serious, chronic illnesses, affecting more than 50 million people in the United States alone. And women are three times more likely to suffer these illnesses than men. I'm one of those women, so I was especially motivated to develop gluten-free baking that matched my discriminating desire for great-tasting pastries.

Since I started eating gluten-free eight years ago, I've noticed drastic improvements in my energy level, mood, and memory, and my quality of life has improved. I'm sure there are many people who've noticed the positive difference a gluten-free lifestyle can have, even without a corroborating medical diagnosis.

I find that some bakers are perplexed about how to keep gluten-free pastries together without going to the opposite end, and they wind up making dense, unchewable "health food" desserts.

But if you unlock the secrets of gluten-free baking, you won't need the glue of gluten. You can make and serve mouthwatering, multi-layered, flavorful pastries held together by the secret ingredient: love.

Love will inspire you to spend the time to mix up the right ingredients that will get you kudos *and* be safe for the gluten-avoiders that you care about. Love will allow *everyone* to embrace celebration cake and come together by sharing the same desserts and pastries. And love will move you to read this book and come back to it as a reference many times for all kinds of special (or just daily) events.

In this book, I'll share many of my discoveries and secrets with you. And I know you're going to love the results.

The Recipes

Most of the recipes in this book are for everyday treats, but a few recipes take a bit more planning and forethought. I start the book off with—you guessed it—breakfast pastries! It's quicker to whip up a batch of your own gluten-free muffins than it is to search all over town to find one you can safely eat, and it will also taste better than something that has been prewrapped and sitting on the store shelf for weeks.

The second chapter discusses the much-beloved fruit desserts—buckles, shortcakes, cobblers, and crisps—and guides you through the differences among these desserts. Best of all, you can mix and match the fillings and toppings for many of these recipes, depending on what's in season, and create entirely new combinations.

The third chapter focuses on a variety of quick breads and coffee cakes, from our popular Lemon Pound Cake (page 40) to Pumpkin Spice Bread (page 39), Sour Cream Coffee Cake (page 35), and a surprisingly spicy-sweet Cornbread with Spicy Honey Butter (page 38).

A fourth chapter covers great comfort foods that are sure to be hits—from easy-but-elegant cookies, brownies, and bar treats to such favorites as S'Mores Tartlets (page 50), Spiced Apple Crumb Bars (page 60), and Mocha Truffle Fudge Brownies (page 45).

A fifth chapter centers on weekend desserts and some spectacular creations that take more preparation or baking time, but are well worth the effort, like Chocolate Mousse Meringue Pie (page 64), Bubbie's Secret Honey Cake (page 63), and mini chocolate chip–studded Cannolizelli (page 73).

Of course, this book wouldn't be complete without a chapter on our bake shop's nationally acclaimed cupcakes, where I highlight our favorites and include some of the more exotic flavors, such as the *Cupcake Wars*–winning African Yam Cupcakes (page 81) and popular Persian Love Cakes (page 93).

I wrap up with a chapter on desserts to impress. These pastries are the perfect party fare, and many of them can be prepared a day ahead of time and set aside until the last minute. Though Mexican Chocolate Baked Alaska (page 99) may at first seem like a complicated dessert, I offer quick tips to speed along the production, without sacrificing any of the qualities inherent in this impressive confection.

Guide to Ingredients and Adjustments

Since I hope this book becomes your ultimate go-to resource, I've included this section on choosing the best ingredients to make it easy for you to recognize the qualities of different grains and starches and perhaps even experiment beyond the recipes in this book. Listed here are just some of the ingredients you'll find in the recipes on these pages. By all means, make adjustments for your diet and what works for you. But remember, because many of us have to individualize what we eat—and some people, like me, are constantly tweaking recipes—substituting ingredients will likely affect the final result. One of my main interests in this book is to familiarize

you with what is available so you can make the best decisions for yourself.

Because I developed these recipes for home bakers, I give volume measurements first ($^1/_4$ cup, $^2/_3$ cup, etc.) However, if you're more comfortable baking by weight (undoubtedly the easiest way to make substitutions and adjustments), feel free to use the conversions given for each ingredient.

EGGS

Eggs are an essential part of fluffy, delicious, gluten-free baking. In addition to the fat eggs provide, they also create structure in the absence of the binding gluten gives to "normal" baked goods. Eggs help bind the dry ingredients and provide height and volume to the final pastry.

I personally am not a fan of egg-replacers in baked goods. That said, you *can* swap out eggs for other substances like ground flaxmeal, but it *will* affect the flavor and the texture. That's not to say it can't be delicious; but it will be different.

The recipes on these pages all refer to large eggs, at room temperature. Eggs that are room temperature and not straight from the refrigerator will combine more easily in batters and doughs. Room-temperature egg whites (around 75°F) will whip up twice as fluffy as cold whites. Eggs require at least a half hour at room temperature to warm up enough to use for baking; if you are short on time, place a whole egg in its shell in a bowl of very warm (but not hot) water for 30 to 60 seconds.

DAIRY

Whenever possible, use the full-fat version of milk, buttermilk, or cream, rather than skim or reduced fat. Not only will the flavor be better, there is also less chance that premium dairy products will contain chemicals or other fillers. You can always apply portion control. A smaller slice of a fully delicious dessert will satisfy you longer than many pieces of reduced-fat pastry.

MILK: I recommend baking with full-fat homogenized milk. If you don't tolerate milk, you can substitute dairy-free alternatives. My favorite is plain (also labeled as "original") rice milk or hemp milk. Steer clear of flavored or vanilla-enhanced varieties: they often contain a lot of sugar and the resulting recipe might be overly sweet. I prefer Pacific Foods Rice Milk or Tempt Hemp Milk.

BUTTERMILK: Buttermilk is usually low fat. In baking, it both adds a tangy zip and tenderizes cakes and pastries. If you need a good dairy-free substitute for buttermilk, put 1 tablespoon of lemon juice in a 1-cup liquid measure and fill with rice milk.

HEAVY WHIPPING CREAM: Most times, you can use full-fat coconut milk as a substitute for heavy whipping cream, but it can affect the flavor and texture of the finished product. Because a "lite" coconut milk will be much more watery than its full-fat cousin, I don't recommend using this for baking. Try Thai Kitchen coconut milk for your dairy-free baking.

FATS

Sometimes vilified as "the bad guy," fat is a terrific flavor enhancer and adds moisture and tenderness to baked goods. Don't be afraid of using fat in these recipes, but be sure to choose the "right" fat—one that accentuates both the texture and flavor of your dessert.

BUTTER: You can't beat the flavor that butter adds to your baking, and, assuming you're not intolerant, or vegan, I recommend using butter whenever possible. The recipes here that call for butter refer to unsalted butter, but if you have salted butter at home, slightly lower the levels of salt in the recipe.

CANOLA OIL: Canola oil is an all-purpose liquid fat and a great alternative to the flavor of coconut oil or shortening if you eat a dairy-free diet. If you're using canola oil as a replacement for butter, you will have to decrease the ratio of other liquids in your recipes accordingly.

COCONUT BUTTER AND COCONUT OIL: The main difference between coconut butter and coconut oil is that the latter is simply the fat (oil) extracted from the coconut meat, while coconut butter is a puree containing some of the coconut meat (flesh and fiber) as well as the fat. I prefer coconut butter.

While you can beat coconut butter like you would beat butter for cookies and cakes, the friction of the beater will likely warm the coconut oil and melt it, so be careful not to beat coconut butter for too long.

Coconut oil adds a slightly sweet and mild tropical flavor to your cakes and scones.

Coconut oil is a saturated fat, which means that, like butter, it's solid at room temperature.

SHORTENING: Organic shortening is another good dairy-free alternative to butter. At the bake shop, we use Spectrum brand because it is vegetarian and has minimal aftertaste.

FLOURS

While cakes, pies, and pastries *can* be made without flour, your baking will be much more versatile, as well as lighter and fluffier, when you use a flour blend. When formulating the recipes in this book, I considered the protein content of various "glutenous" flours and how it affects the resultant pastries. Protein content is much more than just nutrition; it also affects consistency and structure. Did you know that even in the world of traditional "gluten-filled" baking, discriminating pastry chefs use a variety of wheat flours, each with a specific protein content? For example, pastry flour has a relatively low protein content of around 9 percent, which helps make very light, flaky crusts and cookies. In contrast, bagels, made with high-gluten flour, have a protein content of nearly 14 percent, which contributes to the denser, chewy texture. A 5 percent difference may not seem like much, but when you consider the finished product (like piecrust versus bagels), you can see that it results in completely different textures. In light of this, I opted *not* to create a one-texture-fits-all baking mix. Rather, I tailored each recipe according to the desired texture of the finished product.

I use Bob's Red Mill brand for all my gluten-free flours and binders. Their website has a wealth of information, including a breakdown of xanthan gum versus guar gum, which you can find here: www.bobsredmill.com/blog/gluten-free/guar-gum-vs-xanthan-gum.

MILLET FLOUR: Millet flour comes from an ancient grain that is similar in protein content to wheat, which makes it ideal for recipes requiring a heartier texture, like Orange-Currant Scones (page 17). Millet flour has a slightly nutty taste and a lovely pale yellow color.

POTATO STARCH: Potato starch should not be confused with the much denser and heavier potato flour. Potato starch is a very fine, light powder with a neutral flavor. Because it absorbs and retains moisture, it is ideal for baking light, fluffy cakes. Before I went gluten-free, I used to substitute up to $1/4$ cup of potato starch for all-purpose flour, so this was one of the first gluten-free flours that I was really excited about using on a regular basis.

SORGHUM FLOUR: Sorghum flour has more protein than most gluten-free starches. It has a slightly sweet flavor but can yield dry and crumbly desserts. Because sorghum flour absorbs liquids rather well, if you are substituting it for other gluten-free flours in your recipes, consider adding extra liquid or fat to your batters and doughs.

SWEET WHITE RICE FLOUR (also known as Mochiko Sticky Rice): Sweet white rice flour is made by grinding glutinous sticky rice rather than all-purpose white rice. Sticky rice has a tackier feel than long-grain white rice when wet, and retains moisture better. The slight gumminess makes it an ideal background ingredient in baked goods where you want a little give, as in ladyfinger sponge for Tiramisu (page 119). The slight tackiness means that when you bake with sweet white rice flour, you can use fewer binding agents.

TAPIOCA STARCH (also known as Tapioca Flour): Tapioca starch is a finely ground powder that feels silky (similar to cornstarch) but doesn't tend to clump. It absorbs moisture well and is light and fluffy, rendering it ideal for creating desserts that have a tender texture. Tapioca starch is clear and shiny when cooked, making it a wonderful thickener for fruit pie fillings.

WHITE RICE FLOUR: White rice flour has a mild flavor and adds crunch to pastries and cookies. Due to its grittier texture, it can create an undesirable sandy texture if overused. I use white rice flour extensively in this book and refer to it simply as "rice flour."

BINDERS

Gluten is the protein largely responsible for contributing to structure and providing elasticity in baked goods. When you start baking gluten-free, you quickly realize two things: (1) there is no single gluten-free perfect flour that you can just substitute for regular all-purpose white flour; and (2) for an ideal texture, you must add extra protein or a binder of some sort. My recipes contain a bit of both.

XANTHAN GUM: Xanthan gum is a stabilizer and thickener often used in gluten-free baking, as well as in sauces, salad dressings, and soups. Be careful not to overwork doughs and batters with xanthan gum already added; the more you work xanthan gum, the more powerful the binding effects become. Too much xanthan gum in a baked good tends to result in a slimy, gummy, marshmallowy texture and can leach the flavor out.

Xanthan gum is most commonly a derivative of corn. People who are sensitive to corn products might consider replacing the xanthan gum in any recipe with an equal amount of ground psyllium seed husk.

PSYLLIUM SEED HUSK POWDER: Also known as powdered fiber, psyllium seed has tremendous binding properties and can be used one-to-one in place of xanthan gum in baking. Psyllium seed husk powder is known for producing a spongy (rather than stretchy) texture. You can find it in the supplements aisle of the grocery store. Look for the powder (or buy the husks and grind into a powder yourself).

OTHER GLUTEN-FREE INGREDIENTS FOR BAKING

AMARANTH FLOUR: Amaranth flour is higher in protein than most of the other gluten-free flours; it has an earthy flavor and a pale brown color. You won't find it in any of the recipes in this book because I don't like the flavor, but feel free to substitute it for some of the other higher-protein flours, like millet or sorghum.

BROWN RICE FLOUR: Brown rice flour has a higher protein content than white rice flour because it contains rice bran. It therefore needs slightly more liquid in the recipe than white rice flour. If used as the predominant flour in baking, brown rice flour can have a sandy or gritty texture.

POTATO FLOUR: Potato flour is made from dehydrating and grinding up potatoes. The resulting flour, while a good thickener in gravies and soups, can taste bitter and lead to dense, heavy baked goods. No surprise, none of my recipes include potato flour.

QUINOA FLOUR: Quinoa flour has a mild nutty flavor, similar to that of millet flour. And quinoa, like millet, is higher in protein than most other gluten-free flours. A bonus: it also has a lovely creamy yellow color. One downside—quinoa flour costs nearly triple the price of millet flour, so I haven't included it in recipes here.

TEFF FLOUR: Teff flour has a mild nutty and earthy flavor. It's darker in color and has a heavier texture than the starchy flours, making it ideal when you want a whole-grain flavor.

GUAR GUM: Guar gum is said to have almost eight times the thickening power of cornstarch. Whereas xanthan gum is known for providing a stretchier texture to baked goods, guar gum is reputed to provide a spongier texture. When excessive guar gum is used, it can lend a bitter flavor to desserts. Guar gum is also high in cellulose, an indigestible fiber. Those with sensitive gastrointestinal tracts might want to avoid it.

Chef's Tips and Baking Secrets

Extraordinary baking is both a science and an art. The science comes from knowing your tools and ingredients; the art, from understanding—and even sensing—how different combinations might interact and how to adjust what you do for different desired results. This is especially true of gluten-free baking. I have a few secrets that will help you make outstanding gluten-free goodies.

Preheat the oven (and try baking your cake a bit hotter than you normally would). I have a chocolate cake that is delicious, but it needs to bake in an oven that is set 25 degrees hotter than if I were using all-purpose flour with gluten. The hot oven means that the butter releases its water as steam and helps the cake rise immediately. This counteracts the common fallacy that gluten-free baked goods are necessarily denser than their glutened counterparts. Don't settle for this: it doesn't have to be true!

Eggs and butter at room temperature are much easier to work with. If you forget to leave the butter out, you can cheat by microwaving it for 7 to 12 seconds. You don't want it to melt, but you do want it just pliable. And you can dip cold eggs into a bowl of warm water for 30 to 60 seconds to warm them. If creaming butter and sugar together, make sure they get really light and fluffy before you add your next ingredients. While it can take as much as 10 minutes for this step, it yields a lighter, fluffier cake and is well worth the extra time.

Go easy on yourself and be adaptable. The recipes in this book have all been tested multiple times. I wanted them to make sense to you and to be as straightforward as possible. That said, if you are relatively new to baking gluten-free, it can still be tricky to let go of what you have been taught about baking with flour. So if a recipe doesn't turn out the way you had envisioned it, see what you can do to salvage it. Can you top the dessert with meringue and toast it to hide cracks or imperfections in the pie? Can you dust the top of the brownies with confectioners' sugar to hide lumps stemming from a less-than-smooth frosting? Bakeries use these little tricks every day to dress up a plain pastry or hide the part of a cookie that might have been pricked by a toothpick.

Never refrigerate for more than two hours when making a dough that is largely comprised of millet flour and butter, like the crumble topping for the Apple Crisp (page 32). In fact, don't even let it sit at room temperature for that long. There's something about the combination of those two ingredients that causes the mixture to smell (and subsequently taste) like cheddar cheese crackers. If you must make the topping or piecrust ahead of time, simply wrap with plastic wrap and freeze. In general, it is better to freeze than refrigerate gluten-free baked goods. Freezing essentially halts spoiling in its tracks. Refrigeration also pulls moisture out of the pastry, whereas leaving the item wrapped in an airtight container at room temperature (if it doesn't have to be chilled) or freezing does not. Once a millet flour–heavy item has been baked, like scones, the best thing to do is eat it all up! Or, barring that, wrap in an airtight container and freeze, pulling out one each time you want to eat it.

Get to know your flours—and how these match with your personal preferences. Some flours I don't use, not because they don't work but because I personally don't care for the flavor. So if you don't tolerate potato starch, or you think tapioca starch tastes metallic and funny, feel free to replace those ingredients with a different starch, like arrowroot or cornstarch. Just because I don't use it in these recipes doesn't mean it's bad. With that said, there *are* reasons why I choose certain flour combinations. To achieve the best results, I've carefully mirrored the protein content of the glutenous flour a master baker would typically use in the gluten-free starches and flours used here.

Experiment! Before I became a pastry chef, I was one of those people who preferred to color inside the lines. I never wanted to try anything new for fear of failing—or worse, letting other people down. Once I went gluten-free, I realized I had to let those fears go. The common wisdom that said baking gluten-free was so difficult actually made experimenting easier for me. If the pros out there had trouble baking gluten-free, then it was okay if I also had challenges. And it was only through experimenting that I stumbled on some of my most delicious pastries! Our super-flaky piecrust was originally *supposed* to be puff pastry. It didn't work out as I had planned for puff pastry, but makes the best piecrust I have ever had, so it was still a success.

Use the best-quality ingredients you can find. Chefs always admonish you to use good-quality wine for cooking to achieve the best results; similarly—especially when baking gluten-free—you want to use the best-quality butter, chocolate, cream, and vanilla that you can get your hands on. The resulting dessert will taste better—richer, yummier, with more depth of flavor—when you use supreme ingredients. Remember that gluten-free baking at its highest level can be tricky (this is why there are so many health-food-tasting gluten-free pastries.) You'll put the odds in your favor of getting great results by not cutting corners on ingredients.

Take shortcuts. Any of the cake-based recipes in this book can be made faster and easier with the use of an all-purpose gluten-free baking mix. Simply substitute the flour blends in my recipes cup for cup with the gluten-free mix. Check to see if your preblended mix contains salt, xanthan gum, and leavenings; you might have to omit the baking powder, salt, and xanthan gum from your recipe. Depending on the blend you use, you will have varying results. I especially like Thomas Keller's Cup4Cup (which does not contain xanthan gum or baking powder), Pamela's Ultimate Gluten-Free Baking Mix, and Bisquick Gluten-Free (both of which do already have the gum and leavening included). For best results, look for a mix that does not contain pea, garbanzo (chickpea), or fava bean flour.

Happy baking!

Muffins and Scones

HOW LESS SUGAR CAN BE MORE

Freshly baked pastries make it bearable to arise on cold winter mornings when all is quiet and still. I slip my feet into my fuzzy slippers and gently pad down the hallway into the kitchen, lightly scented from my baking the day before. I select a scone studded with plump currants or a toothsome rice bran muffin, and slice horizontally into it. With a wodge of butter sizzling in a small saucepan, I lay the muffin cut side down and heat until it's toasty and buttery. I pour myself a cup of coffee and sit at my kitchen table watching the steam rise off the neighbor's roof as I nibble on my breakfast and think about the daily menu at the shop.

Someone once told me they didn't like muffins because they thought of them as just naked cupcakes. However, if baked well, muffins should be far less sweet than an undressed cupcake, and a great way to start the morning without overspiking your blood sugar. Likewise with scones. Somewhere between a biscuit and a shortbread cookie, scones are lightly sweetened, a little crunchy around the edges, and the perfect complement to a piping hot cup of tea.

BRAN(LESS) MUFFINS

{EASY}   Makes 15 muffins

As a child, I was afraid of bran muffins. They just sounded so *healthy*. Ironically, about the time I went gluten-free, bran muffins started sounding tasty to me, but of course I couldn't eat them. I was very motivated to develop this recipe, using cream of rice cereal in place of the wheat bran. If you eat these muffins warmed in a pan with butter, the butter melts into the muffin and turns it golden brown, crisp, and extra delicious.

¹/₂ cup / 91 g cream of rice cereal

³/₄ cup / 136 g raisins (optional)

³/₄ cup / 177 ml boiling water

¹/₄ cup packed / 63 g golden brown sugar

2 eggs

¹/₂ cup / 108 g canola or grapeseed oil

¹/₂ cup / 170 g molasses

¹/₂ cup / 89 g sweet white rice flour

¹/₄ cup / 36 g sorghum flour

1 cup / 130 g tapioca starch

³/₄ cup / 142 g potato starch

1 teaspoon / 4.6 g baking soda

1 teaspoon / 5 g baking powder

¹/₂ teaspoon / .5 g xanthan gum

¹/₂ teaspoon / 2.4 g salt

¹/₂ cup / 113 ml buttermilk

1 teaspoon / 5 g vanilla extract

Preheat the oven to 325°F. Line one 12-cup muffin pan and 3 cups from a second muffin pan with paper liners and set aside.

Measure out the cereal and the raisins into a small bowl and pour the boiling water over the top. Stir once to combine and set aside.

In a large mixing bowl, stir together the sugar, eggs, and oil. Stir in the molasses. In a separate bowl, combine the flours, starches, baking soda, baking powder, xanthan gum, and salt. Add half of this mixture to the large mixing bowl and stir to combine. Stir in the buttermilk and vanilla, then add the remaining flour mixture. Add the cereal mixture, including any water that has not been absorbed, and mix into the batter.

Evenly fill the muffin cups three-quarters full and bake until a toothpick inserted in the center comes out clean, 12 to 16 minutes.

Remove from the muffin pans onto a cooling rack and enjoy warm or cool.

ORANGE-CURRANT SCONES

{EASY}   Makes 18 scones

Like a lot of little girls, I loved to have tea parties, with my stuffed animals as guests (I called them "my people"). When I was eight, my mom took me to see *The Nutcracker*, and we went to high tea at Portland's Heathman Hotel beforehand. There were brownies and lemon tartlets on the three-tiered platter, but it was the currant scones with strawberry jam and clotted cream that got my attention. Each time I eat these scones, I close my eyes and remember the magic of that ultimate tea party.

1 cup / 170 g sweet white rice flour

1 cup / 147 g millet flour

1 cup / 190 g potato starch

1 cup / 130 g tapioca starch

²/₃ cup / 151 g sugar

1 tablespoon / 3 g xanthan gum

1 tablespoon / 14 g baking powder

1 teaspoon / 4.7 g salt

¹/₂ teaspoon / 2.4 g baking soda

2 tablespoons / 21 g finely chopped orange zest (from about 2 medium-sized oranges)

³/₄ cup / 110 g dried currants

³/₄ cup / 170 g cold butter, diced into large cubes

¹/₄ cup / 57 ml orange juice

1 cup / 238 ml heavy cream

ORANGE GLAZE

4 cups / 568 g confectioners' sugar

¹/₂ cup / 113 ml orange juice

Preheat the oven to 300°F. Line a baking sheet with parchment paper and set aside.

· In a large bowl, stir together the flours, starches, sugar, xanthan gum, baking powder, salt, and baking soda. Add the orange zest and dried currants and stir to combine. Using a pastry blender or your fingertips, mix the butter into the dry ingredients until the mixture resembles coarse pea-sized crumbs. Pour the orange juice and the cream over the flour mixture and stir to distribute through the dough. Dough should come together if you squeeze a handful of it, but should not feel excessively wet. Make sure there are no loose dry ingredients at the bottom of the bowl and that everything is well combined.

Divide the dough into 3 equal portions and flatten each portion into a disk about 7 inches across by ¹/₂ inch high. Cut each disk in half and then cut each half into 3 equal wedges. Arrange evenly on the baking sheet and bake until set, 30 to 35 minutes. If you gently squeeze the sides of the scone, there should be a little resistance, but they should not feel squishy. Let the scones cool on the baking sheet.

To make the glaze, whisk together the confectioners' sugar and orange juice until smooth and shiny. Liberally drizzle the glaze on top of each scone and let it set, 30 to 60 minutes.

CHOCOLATE CHOCOLATE-CHIP MUFFINS

{EASY}   Makes 15 muffins

One day our sweet counter girl, Chelsea, was watching me develop the Almond Biscotti recipe (page 57) and started lamenting how her grandmother used to make chocolate chocolate-chip muffins for her when she was little; but ever since Chelsea had gone gluten-free, she hadn't been able to eat one. Well, Chelsea—this one's for you! These keep incredibly well if you wrap them individually and freeze them in an airtight container.

½ cup / 113 g butter

½ cup / 113 g granulated sugar

½ cup packed / 127 g brown sugar

4 eggs

⅔ cup / 57 g cocoa powder

½ cup / 95 g potato starch

½ cup / 67 g tapioca starch

⅓ cup / 55 g rice flour

1 tablespoon plus 1 teaspoon / 19 g baking powder

½ teaspoon / 2.4 g salt

1¼ teaspoon / .3 g xanthan gum

½ cup / 108 ml canola oil

⅔ cup / 151 ml milk

2 teaspoons / 10 g vanilla extract

½ cup / 85 g mini chocolate chips

Preheat the oven to 350°F. Line one 12-cup muffin pan and 3 cups from a second muffin pan with paper liners and set aside.

Using a stand mixer with a paddle attachment, cream the butter on high speed until light and fluffy, about 6 minutes. Add the sugars and beat until creamy and light. Add the eggs one at a time, and blend thoroughly, stopping occasionally to scrape down the sides of the bowl.

In a separate bowl, combine the cocoa powder, starches, rice flour, baking powder, salt, and xanthan gum. Add a third of the dry mixture to the butter mixture and blend on low speed until mostly combined. Add the oil and mix until blended. Mix in half of the remaining dry mixture, stopping occasionally to scrape down the sides of the bowl. Blend in half of the milk, then the remaining flour mixture, and then the rest of the milk and the vanilla. Stir in the mini chocolate chips by hand.

Evenly fill the muffin cups three-quarters full and bake until a toothpick inserted in the center comes out clean, 14 to 20 minutes.

Remove from the muffin pans onto a cooling rack and let cool completely before serving.

CHERRY WHITE-CHOCOLATE SCONES

{EASY} Makes 18 scones

My dad is a chocoholic, and that includes white chocolate (technically not chocolate at all, but sweetened cocoa butter). He often traveled for work and would bring back chocolates from his travels. One of his favorites was something we called an "Oh My God Bar." I don't remember the brand, but it was so good that whenever we ate it, we would roll our eyes into the back of our heads and moan, "Oh. My. God." Coated with white chocolate, the middle was filled with a hazelnut milk chocolate. My dad would cut each bar into eight pieces and serve it after dinner on a plate with Rainier cherries picked from the tree outside our kitchen window. Those storied after-dinner snacks have inspired this breakfast scone.

1 cup / 170 g sweet white rice flour

1 cup / 147 g millet flour

1 cup / 190 g potato starch

1 cup / 130 g tapioca starch

2/3 cup / 151 g sugar

1 tablespoon / 3 g xanthan gum

1 tablespoon / 14 g baking powder

1/2 teaspoon / 2.4 g baking soda

1 teaspoon / 4.7 g salt

1/2 cup / 71 g dried cherries, diced

1/4 cup / 44 g good-quality white chocolate, chopped into small pieces

3/4 cup / 170 g cold butter, diced into large cubes

1 1/2 cups / 357 ml heavy cream

1 teaspoon / 5 g vanilla extract

GLAZE

4 cups / 568 g confectioners' sugar

1/2 cup / 113 ml whole milk

1/2 teaspoon / 2.5 g vanilla extract

Preheat the oven to 300°F. Line a baking sheet with parchment paper and set aside.

In a large bowl, stir together the flours, starches, sugar, xanthan gum, baking powder, baking soda, and salt. Add the cherries and white chocolate and stir to combine. Using a pastry blender or your fingertips, mix the butter into the dry ingredients until the mixture resembles coarse pea-sized crumbs. Pour the cream and vanilla over the flour mixture and stir to distribute through the dough. Dough should come together if you squeeze a handful of it, but should not feel excessively wet. Make sure there are no loose dry ingredients at the bottom of the bowl and that everything is well combined.

Divide the dough into 3 equal portions and flatten each portion into a disk about 7 inches across by 1/2 inch high. Cut each disk in half and then cut each half into 3 equal wedges. Arrange evenly on the baking sheet and bake until set, 30 to 35 minutes. If you gently squeeze the sides of the scone, there should be a little resistance, but they should not feel squishy. Let the scones cool on the baking sheet.

To make the glaze, whisk together the confectioners' sugar, milk, and vanilla until smooth and shiny. Drizzle the glaze on top of each cooled scone and let it set, 30 to 60 minutes.

ESPRESSO SCONES

{EASY}   Makes 18 scones

The summer after I turned sixteen was magical. I had my driver's license, which meant freedom, and my friend Beth and I spent many humid evenings sitting in the garden at the Pied Cow in southeast Portland, an old Victorian house converted into a funky, velvet-wallpapered coffeeshop that served up cups of cappuccino alongside espresso scones. Whenever I taste the sweet coffee bite of these buttery bittersweet scones, I am transported to those days of newfound independence and endless possibilities.

1 cup / 170 g sweet white rice flour

1 cup / 147 g millet flour

1 cup / 190 g potato starch

1 cup / 130 g tapioca starch

²/₃ cup / 151 g sugar

1 tablespoon / 3 g xanthan gum

1 tablespoon / 14 g baking powder

¹/₂ teaspoon / 2.4 g baking soda

1 teaspoon / 4.7 g salt

3 tablespoons / 16 g dried espresso powder

³/₄ cup / 170 g cold butter, diced into large cubes

1¹/₂ cups / 357 ml heavy cream

1 teaspoon / 5 g vanilla extract

ESPRESSO GLAZE

4 cups / 568 g confectioners' sugar

¹/₂ cup / 113 ml whole milk

2 tablespoons / 8.5 g espresso powder

Preheat the oven to 300°F. Line a baking sheet with parchment paper and set aside.

In a large bowl, stir together the flours, starches, sugar, xanthan gum, baking powder, baking soda, and salt. Add the espresso powder and stir to combine. Using a pastry blender or your fingertips, mix the butter into the dry ingredients until the mixture resembles coarse pea-sized crumbs. Pour 1¹/₄ cups of the cream and the vanilla over the flour mixture and stir to distribute through the dough. Dough should come together if you squeeze a handful of it, but should not feel excessively wet. Make sure there are no loose dry ingredients at the bottom of the bowl and that everything is well combined.

Divide the dough into 3 equal portions and flatten each portion into a disk about 7 inches across by ¹/₂ inch high. Cut each disk in half and then cut each half into 3 equal wedges. Arrange evenly on the baking sheet and brush the tops of each scone with the remaining ¹/₄ cup of cream. Bake until set, 30 to 35 minutes. If you gently squeeze the sides of the scone, there should be a little resistance, but they should not feel squishy. Let the scones cool completely on the baking sheet.

To make the glaze, whisk together the confectioners' sugar, milk, and espresso powder until smooth and shiny. Top each scone with a tablespoonful of glaze and let set, 30 to 60 minutes.

Buckles, Cobblers, and Crisps

When I was first dating my husband Jason, we headed out of town for a weekend away and found ourselves winding along the Oregon Coast Highway. Rain lashed against the windshield, and even with the wipers on overdrive, there were scary moments when we couldn't see the road.

We stopped at a restaurant overlooking the foamy gray ocean waves, hoping to sit out the worst of the storm and warm up. I don't remember much about my meal, but dessert is etched in my memory: a steaming bowl of marionberry cobbler and hot coffee.

Cobbler toppings can differ greatly: on this particular Oregon Coast cobbler, the berries were still intact and only slightly sweet; blanketing the marionberries was a soft, cakelike topping that tasted like a doughnut. We dipped our spoons into the warm dessert and melting vanilla ice cream, ignoring the pounding rain outside and falling in love with the cobbler, and each other.

In this chapter, I invite you to fall in love with your own favorite fruit dessert, whether it's made with strawberries, blueberries, apples, or yes, marionberries.

GRAMMA TISHIE'S STRAWBERRY RHUBARB COBBLER

{EASY}   Makes 12 servings

My great-grandmother was from the Deep South. She preferred lard to butter any day, and had an inherent love of cornbread, corn cake, and dessert with every meal. I took the inspiration from a meal I had at a restaurant in New Orleans and created this dessert in Gramma Tishie's honor. Because it's not overly sweet, the better to add a scoop of vanilla bean ice cream or blood orange sorbet!

These days, lard is more difficult to find in grocery stores, so I've replaced it with butter in the corn cake topping. If you have a dairy allergy, feel free to give lard (or coconut butter) a try. If you're using fresh rhubarb, be sure to remove any stringy strands from the stalks.

4 cups / 538 g fresh or frozen rhubarb, chopped into 1/2-inch pieces

2 heaping cups / 340 g strawberries, hulled and quartered

3/4 cup / 170 g sugar

2 tablespoons / 16 g tapioca starch

1/4 cup / 57 ml orange juice

1 teaspoon / 3.5 g orange zest

CORN CAKE TOPPING

1/2 cup / 113 g butter, room temperature

1/3 cup / 76 g sugar

2 eggs

3/4 cup / 102 g finely ground cornmeal

3/4 cup / 122 g sweet white rice flour

1/2 cup / 67 g tapioca starch

1 tablespoon / 14 g baking powder

1/2 teaspoon / 2.4 g salt

1/2 cup / 113 ml orange juice

Preheat the oven to 325°F. Spray an 8-inch square baking pan with gluten-free cooking spray and set aside.

In a saucepan over medium-low heat, stir together the rhubarb, strawberries, sugar, tapioca starch, orange juice, and orange zest and heat, stirring occasionally, until the fruit juice mixture thickens slightly and the sugar dissolves, about 12 minutes.

Meanwhile, assemble the topping. Using a stand mixer with a paddle attachment, cream together the butter and sugar on high speed until light and fluffy, about 5 minutes. Add the eggs, one at a time, and blend thoroughly, stopping occasionally to scrape down the sides of the bowl. In a separate bowl, combine the cornmeal, rice flour, tapioca starch, baking powder, and salt. Add half of the cornmeal mixture to the butter mixture and mix on low speed to mostly combine. Blend in the orange juice and then the remaining cornmeal mixture. The batter should be thick.

Pour the rhubarb filling into the baking pan and cover with dollops of the corn cake mixture. Bake until golden brown and a toothpick inserted in the center comes out clean, about 25 minutes. This cobbler is fantastic served hot or cold the day it's made.

TRIPLE BERRY COBBLER

Because this is one of my all-time favorite desserts, I often bring a large casserole dish of it to share at potlucks and barbecues. Despite the long cooking time, it's very quick to throw together and is always a crowd-pleaser. If there's a wholesale club near you, look for the 3-pound bags of mixed frozen berries—although fresh is always great during the height of summer! The cornmeal in this batter lends the cobbler a satisfying crunch and contrasts nicely with the warm, soft berries. I like to serve this with homemade vanilla bean ice cream or lightly sweetened whipped cream.

About 2²/₃ cups / 454 g blueberries

About 2²/₃ cups / 454 g raspberries

About 2¹/₂ cups / 454 g marionberries

1¹/₄ cups / 284 g sugar

¹/₄ cup / 37 g cornstarch

¹/₄ cup / 57 ml lemon juice

TOPPING

1 cup / 227 g butter, room temperature

1 cup / 227 g sugar

1 tablespoon / 14 g vanilla extract

²/₃ cup / 91 g cornmeal

²/₃ cup / 85 g tapioca starch

¹/₃ cup / 63 g potato starch

¹/₃ cup / 55 g rice flour

1 tablespoon plus 1 teaspoon / 19 g baking powder

1 teaspoon / 4.7 g salt

1 teaspoon / 2.6 g cinnamon

¹/₂ teaspoon / 1 g cardamom

¹/₄ teaspoon / .3 g xanthan gum

1 cup / 227 ml milk

2 tablespoons / 28 g coarse sanding sugar or granulated sugar, for topping

Preheat the oven to 375°F.

In a large bowl, toss together the blueberries, raspberries, marionberries, sugar, cornstarch, and lemon juice to evenly coat the berries. Pour into a 9 by 13-inch baking pan.

To make the topping, using a stand mixer with a paddle attachment, cream together the butter and sugar until light and fluffy. Blend in the vanilla. In a separate bowl, combine the cornmeal, starches, rice flour, baking powder, salt, cinnamon, cardamom, and xanthan gum. Add the dry ingredients to the butter mixture in 3 additions, alternating with the milk.

Pour the topping over the berry filling. Sprinkle the sanding sugar evenly over the topping and bake until the topping is cooked through, a toothpick inserted in the center comes out clean, and the berry filling is hot and bubbly, 65 to 70 minutes. Cover the dish with foil if the top browns too quickly. Serve hot or cold.

BLUEBERRY BUCKLE BREAKFAST CAKE

{EASY}   Makes 9 large servings

When I was growing up, my dad and I would get up early on Saturday mornings and drive to a nearby "u-pick" farm that had acres of blueberry bushes. We would race to see who could fill their bucket the fastest: he was a better picker but ate the berries by the handful, whereas I picked straight into the bucket. They would weigh our buckets and we'd pay by the pound (they really should have weighed my dad before and after picking!). We would return to the cool air-conditioning of our house and make this breakfast cake to enjoy some of our hard-earned bounty.

1/2 cup / 113 g butter, room temperature

1 1/2 cups / 371 g brown sugar

1/4 cup / 57 g granulated sugar

1 egg

2/3 cup / 85 g tapioca starch

2/3 cup / 127 g potato starch

2/3 cup / 111 g rice flour

2 teaspoons / 10 g baking powder

1/2 teaspoon / 2.4 g salt

1/4 teaspoon / .3 g xanthan gum

2/3 cup / 151 ml milk

1/2 teaspoon / 2.5 g vanilla extract

1 1/2 cups / 255 g fresh or frozen blueberries

TOPPING

1/4 cup / 57 g butter, room temperature

1/3 cup packed / 71 g brown sugar

1/4 cup / 47 g potato starch

1/4 cup / 40 g rice flour

1/2 teaspoon / 1.3 g ground cinnamon

1/8 teaspoon / .3 g ground cloves

Preheat the oven to 350°F. Spray an 8-inch square baking pan with gluten-free cooking spray and set aside.

Using a stand mixer with a paddle attachment, cream the butter until it is light and fluffy. Slowly add the sugars and beat several more minutes on high speed until creamy and pale in color. Add the egg and blend thoroughly. In a separate bowl, combine the starches, rice flour, baking powder, salt, and xanthan gum. Add the dry ingredients to the butter mixture in 3 additions, alternating with the milk, and blend thoroughly with each addition. Stir in the vanilla. Pour the batter into the baking pan and bake for 25 to 30 minutes to set the batter.

To make the topping, mix together the butter, brown sugar, potato starch, rice flour, cinnamon, and cloves until crumbly.

Once the batter is set, remove the cake from the oven and sprinkle the blueberries and then the crumb topping over the batter. Bake until golden brown and a toothpick inserted in the center comes out clean, 25 to 30 minutes more. Let cool about 30 minutes and then cut into squares and enjoy.

STRAWBERRY SHORTCAKE

{EASY}   Makes 12 servings (unless I'm one of the twelve: in that case, this recipe will serve 2)

There are many types of strawberry shortcake—biscuity, pound-cakey, angel food–cakey—but they all have two things in common: the lightly sweetened berries and clouds of whipped cream. I have always preferred the biscuity type, and often made these for dinner when I was in college. I couldn't afford to buy groceries for both dinner and dessert, so, like a good little future pastry chef, I often just skipped dinner (bet you aren't surprised).

The biscuit bottoms of this shortcake provide crunch and melt-in-your-mouth butteriness and make you feel as if you're eating something vaguely healthy. I like my fruit to taste like fruit, so the berry mix has minimal refined sugar; I use orange juice for natural flavor and sweetness. The whipped cream is the kicker—if you're like me and *really* like whipped cream, then double the amount called for. You can make the shortcakes up to a week ahead of time—just freeze them in an airtight container. Simply refresh them in a 300°F oven for 3 to 5 minutes. This is a fantastic dessert for summer dinner parties when strawberries are in their sweetest and juiciest prime.

SHORTCAKES

3/4 cup / 110 g millet flour

1/2 cup / 89 g rice flour

1/2 cup / 67 g tapioca starch

1/4 cup / 47 g potato starch

2/3 cup / 151 g sugar

1 tablespoon / 14 g baking powder

2 teaspoons / 7 g orange zest

1 teaspoon / 4.7 g salt

1/2 teaspoon / .5 g xanthan gum

1/4 teaspoon / 1.2 g baking soda

6 tablespoons / 76 g butter, cold and cubed

3/4 cup / 178 ml heavy cream

2 tablespoons / 30 g sanding sugar, for topping

Preheat the oven to 350°F. Line a baking sheet with parchment paper and set aside.

To make the shortcakes, mix together the flours, starches, sugar, baking powder, orange zest, salt, xanthan gum, and baking soda. Using your fingertips (or a food processor), mix the butter into the dry ingredients until the mixture resembles coarse pea-sized crumbs. Add the cream and combine just until moistened. Spoon 12 golf ball–sized lumps 3 inches apart on the baking sheet and press gently to flatten. Shortcakes will spread during baking. Sprinkle about 1/2 teaspoon of the topping sugar over each shortcake and bake until lightly golden brown around the edges and a toothpick inserted in the center comes out clean, 12 to 18 minutes.

Remove from the oven and let cool completely.

ingredients and method continued

STRAWBERRY TOPPING

2 pints fresh strawberries

1 tablespoon / 14 g sugar

2 tablespoons / 21 g orange zest

1/4 cup / 57 ml fresh-squeezed
orange juice

WHIPPED CREAM

2 cups / 476 ml heavy whipping
cream

1/4 cup / 37 g confectioners' sugar

1/4 cup / 57 ml orange juice

Rinse and drain the berries. Slice off the stems and cut into 1/4-inch slices, or cut in half before slicing if the berries are very large. Place the sliced berries in a bowl, sprinkle with the sugar and the orange zest, and gently stir to coat. Pour the orange juice over the strawberries and chill until ready to serve, up to 4 hours.

To make the whipped cream, chill a mixing bowl and add the cream, confectioners' sugar, and orange juice. Whip on medium-high speed until thick and fluffy and medium peaks hold.

To serve, place one shortcake at the bottom of a small bowl. Stir the berries to mix them up with the juice, and divide the berries and the juice among the bowls. Place a dollop of whipped cream on top of the berry stack and devour!

MARIONBERRY CRISPLER

{EASY}   Makes about 12 servings

Sometimes when a dessert doesn't work out as planned, you stumble on another gem. My husband and I were staying with our dear friends Rob and Amy at her aunt and uncle's home on Whidbey Island. It was a crisp, gray January weekend, and on our last night, Amy and I decided to make dinner as a thank you. Aunt Peg had pounds of marionberries, picked from her garden at the peak of purple ripeness and frozen, so I thought I'd make a crisp. Unfortunately, I couldn't find oats, or gluten-free flour, or most of what I'd normally use. I delivered my disclaimer while we were eating dinner, and Rob was suspicious of any food that might be "healthy," including anything gluten-free. However, when he tasted the dessert, he proclaimed it an awesome "crispler" and declared that he now loved gluten-free desserts. In honor of all the Robs out there, here's the recipe! (Note: Udi's Pure & Simple Au Naturel Granola or Purely Elizabeth Original Granola are great low-sugar gluten-free brands.)

CRISPLER TOPPING

1/2 cup / 113 g butter, room temperature

2/3 cup packed / 142 g brown sugar

2 cups / 227 g low-sugar gluten-free granola

2/3 cup / 102 g cornstarch

3 tablespoons / 34 g finely chopped candied or crystallized ginger

1 tablespoon / 7.8 g cinnamon

1/2 teaspoon / 2.4 g salt

MARIONBERRY FILLING

7 1/2 cups / 907 g marionberries, fresh or frozen

2/3 cup / 151 g sugar

1/2 cup / 78 g cornstarch

WHIPPED CREAM

1 cup (1/2 pint) / 238 ml heavy whipping cream

1 tablespoon / 9 g confectioners' sugar

1/2 teaspoon / 2.5 g vanilla extract

Preheat the oven to 350°F.

To make the topping, using a stand mixer with a paddle attachment, cream the butter until light and fluffy. Add the brown sugar and beat until well blended and creamy. Blend in the granola, cornstarch, ginger, cinnamon, and salt and set aside.

To make the filling, in an 8-inch square baking pan, toss together the marionberries, sugar, and cornstarch to evenly coat all the berries.

Evenly crumble the topping over the berries and bake until the topping is golden brown and set and the berry filling is bubbling at the edges, 65 to 75 minutes. (You can assemble and bake the crispler a day ahead and keep it in the refrigerator.)

To make the whipped cream, add the cream, confectioners' sugar, and vanilla to a large mixing bowl and whip on medium-high speed until thick and fluffy and medium peaks hold.

To serve, place a dollop of whipped cream on each serving and enjoy lukewarm, or let cool and serve cold.

APPLE CRISP

When we were first on our own, my friend Kim and I often went back and forth to each other's apartment for dinner. She would always make the most delicious apple crisp for dessert. This is a gluten-free variation on her recipe. Feel free to assemble the apple filling up to 2 days in advance and keep it chilled until you're ready to bake it. Don't make the topping ahead of time, though, unless you plan to freeze the whole thing unbaked; the millet flour and butter combination start tasting faintly Parmesany if combined but left unfrozen for more than 2 hours.

6 large / 906 g tart apples (Pippin or Granny Smith)

$1/3$ cup / 76 g sugar, or $1/4$ cup / 76 g maple syrup

2 tablespoons / 16 g tapioca starch

1 tablespoon / 7.8 g ground cinnamon

$1/2$ teaspoon / 1.1 g Chinese five-spice powder

$1/2$ teaspoon / .9 g ground ginger

Generous pinch / 3.6 g salt

3 tablespoons / 42 g cold butter

TOPPING

$1/2$ cup / 89 g sweet white rice flour

$1/2$ cup / 74 g millet flour

$1/2$ cup / 67 g tapioca starch

1 cup packed / 244 g golden brown sugar

1 teaspoon / 2.6 g ground cinnamon

1 teaspoon / 4.7 g salt

$1/2$ teaspoon / 1.1 g Chinese five-spice powder

$1/2$ teaspoon / .9 g ground ginger

$3/4$ cup / 170 g butter, room temperature

$3/4$ cup / 68 g gluten-free oats

$1/2$ cup / 51 g chopped pecans or walnuts (optional)

Preheat the oven to 350°F.

Peel, core, and slice the apples into $1/4$- inch slices. Put the apple slices into a large bowl and sprinkle the sugar over the top. Add the tapioca starch, cinnamon, five-spice, ginger, and salt and toss together to evenly coat the apple slices. Pour into a 9 by 13-inch baking pan, dot the top with pieces of the butter and set aside.

To make the topping, combine the flours, tapioca starch, brown sugar, cinnamon, salt, five-spice, and ginger in a mixing bowl. In a stand mixer with a paddle attachment, mix in the butter until it is uniformly incorporated into the flour mixture. Stir in the oats and pecans.

Crumble the oat topping evenly over the apples. Bake until the topping is golden brown and set and the apples are warm and bubbly, 55 to 60 minutes.

You can prepare everything ahead of time. Refrigerate the apple filling and keep the topping frozen until ready to assemble and bake. Don't refrigerate the unbaked topping overnight, as the millet flour will interact with the butter and taste and smell cheesy when it's baked.

Quick Breads and Coffee Cakes

CONVERSATION STARTERS

Diving into a freshly baked coffee cake is like sitting down to talk with your best friend: it's both familiar and surprising, deeply comforting but filled with little pockets of sweetness.

Do you have a favorite memory involving quick bread or coffee cake? For me, it's less about eating the cake and more about the scent in the air. My grandmother lived in the mountains of Southern California on a piece of property that had orange, grapefruit, and macadamia nut trees. Whenever I visited, she would make a different type of coffee cake for our breakfast on my first morning there. We'd bring our coffee and a thick slab of macadamia nut or orange-scented cake and half a grapefruit into the shaded backyard to enjoy the fragrance of citrus and wildflowers in the air. Whenever I now catch a whiff of that particular combination, I'm transported back to her yard, with a craving for coffee cake.

SOUR CREAM COFFEE CAKE

{EASY} Makes 12 to 14 servings

Coffee cakes, with their cinnamon crumb topping, have always appealed to me. At coffee shops, I would often order a thick slice, and when I went gluten-free, I was disappointed that my habit would have to stop. The last piece of coffee cake I had before my conversion was for high tea at the Butchart Gardens in Victoria, Canada. I was twenty years old and had been undergoing tests for months on end, with no diagnosis, so my parents scheduled a family vacation to relax me. On our second afternoon, we strolled around the verdant Butchart Gardens and stayed for high tea: piles of mini scones, finger sandwiches, coffee cake, jam, and clotted cream were served, and though I later regretted eating it, it was all delicious. Shortly after our return, I found out I needed to switch to a gluten-free lifestyle. So I created this recipe, using sour cream in the batter for a slight tanginess and a tender crumb. Be sure to look for a sour cream that has no modified food starch added to it.

STREUSEL TOPPING

$^1/_2$ cup / 113 g sugar

$^1/_2$ cup packed / 127 g brown sugar

$^1/_2$ cup / 89 g sweet white rice flour

$^1/_4$ cup / 37 g millet flour

1 tablespoon / 7.8 g cinnamon

$^1/_2$ cup / 113 g butter, cold and cubed

1 cup / 85 g toasted pecans or almonds, coarsely chopped

COFFEE CAKE

$^3/_4$ cup / 170 g butter

1 cup / 227 g sugar

4 large eggs

2 teaspoons / 10 g vanilla extract

1 cup / 190 g potato starch

1 cup / 130 g tapioca starch

1 cup / 170 g rice flour

1 teaspoon / 4.6 g baking soda

1 teaspoon / 4.7 g salt

$^1/_2$ teaspoon / .5 g xanthan gum

12 ounces / 340 g sour cream

Preheat the oven to 325°F. Spray a large (2-pound) loaf pan with gluten-free cooking spray and set aside.

To make the streusel topping, mix together the sugars, flours, and cinnamon. Using your fingertips (or a food processor), mix in the butter until the mixture resembles coarse pea-sized crumbs. Stir in the pecans and set aside.

To make the cake, using a stand mixer with a paddle attachment, cream the butter on high speed until light and fluffy. Scrape down the sides of the bowl and on medium speed slowly add the sugar. Continue beating until light in color and the sugar is fully mixed in. Add the eggs, one at a time, fully incorporating after each addition. Then blend in the vanilla.

In a separate bowl, combine the starches, rice flour, baking soda, salt, and xanthan gum. Add the dry ingredients to the butter mixture in 3 additions, alternating with the sour cream, and blend thoroughly after each addition.

Pour the batter into the loaf pan and sprinkle the streusel mixture over the top. Bake until a toothpick inserted in the center comes out clean, 45 to 50 minutes. Let cool completely. Run a butter knife around the edge of the pan. Turn the coffee cake out of the pan and slice into $^3/_4$- inch slices.

BANANA BREAD

My husband, Jason, is a great cook, but he is not a baker. While he adores banana bread, for some reason I really don't like touching (or eating) raw bananas, so I rarely make anything banana related either at home or at the bake shop. Jason likes this banana bread so much that the few times I make it for him, he refuses to share it with anyone. I'm including the recipe here in hopes that *you* will make this delicious banana bread for Jason so I won't have to!

$^3/_4$ cup / 170 g butter

$^3/_4$ cup / 170 g granulated sugar

$^3/_4$ cup packed / 190 g brown sugar

3 eggs

$1^1/_2$ teaspoons / 7.5 g vanilla extract

$^3/_4$ cup / 142 g potato starch

$^3/_4$ cup / 96 g tapioca starch

$^3/_4$ cup / 122 g rice flour

$1^1/_2$ tablespoons / 21.5 g baking powder

$1^1/_2$ teaspoons / 7 g baking soda

$^3/_4$ teaspoon / 3.6 g fine sea salt

1 tablespoon / 7.8 g cinnamon

$1^3/_4$ teaspoons / 3 g ground ginger

1 teaspoon / 3.5 g orange zest

$^3/_4$ teaspoon / 1.7 g ground nutmeg

$^1/_4$ teaspoon / .5 g ground cloves

6 very ripe medium-sized bananas, mashed (about 3 cups / 675 g banana puree)

Preheat the oven to 350°F. Spray two 1-pound loaf pans with gluten-free cooking spray and set aside.

Using a stand mixer with a paddle attachment, cream the butter and sugars on high speed until light and fluffy, about 5 minutes. Add the eggs, one at a time, and blend thoroughly, stopping occasionally to scrape down the sides of the bowl. Then blend in the vanilla. In a separate bowl, combine the starches, rice flour, baking powder, baking soda, salt, cinnamon, ginger, orange zest, nutmeg, and cloves. Mix in a third of the dry ingredients on low speed until mostly incorporated. Then mix in the second third of the dry ingredients as with the first. Add the mashed bananas and blend into the batter, then mix in the remaining dry ingredients, stopping occasionally to scrape down the sides of the bowl. The batter should be thick.

Pour the batter into the loaf pans and bake until a toothpick inserted in the center comes out clean, 35 to 40 minutes. Let cool completely. Turn out of the pans and do as my husband does: cut into thick slices and slather with butter.

CORNBREAD WITH SPICY HONEY BUTTER

{EASY}   Makes 9 squares

Cannon Beach is on the northern Oregon coast, about an hour's drive from where I live. My husband, Jason, and I like to go there for a long day trip, or a weekend away. Our favorite restaurant is the Lumberyard Grill, known for their amazingly moist rotisserie chicken and sweet skillet cornbread. According to Jason, this is a great gluten-free version of their recipe. While this cornbread is sweet and moist, if you prefer a less-sweet cornbread, simply leave off the honey butter topping. You can add a can of diced jalapeños or 4 ounces of shredded pepperjack cheese (or both!) to the batter for a spicier kick, or omit the cayenne altogether to go mild.

1¼ cups / 170 g coarse stone-ground yellow cornmeal

½ cup / 113 g sugar

⅓ cup / 55 g rice flour

⅓ cup / 41 g tapioca starch

⅓ cup / 63 g potato starch

1 tablespoon / 14 g baking powder

1 teaspoon / 4.7 g coarse kosher salt

½ teaspoon / .9 g cayenne pepper

⅛ teaspoon / .1 g xanthan gum

1 cup / 227 ml buttermilk

¼ cup / 91 g honey

¼ cup / 57 g butter, melted

2 eggs

HONEY BUTTER

½ cup / 113 g butter, room temperature

¼ cup / 91 g honey

¼ teaspoon / .4 g cayenne pepper

Preheat the oven to 350°F. Spray an 8-inch square baking pan with gluten-free cooking spray and line with parchment paper.

In a bowl, combine the cornmeal, sugar, rice flour, starches, baking powder, salt, cayenne, and xanthan gum. Mix in the buttermilk, honey, butter, and eggs.

Pour the batter into the baking pan and bake until a toothpick inserted in the center just comes out clean, 20 to 25 minutes. Remove from the oven and let cool completely. Cut into 9 squares.

Meanwhile, make the honey butter. Using a stand mixer with a paddle attachment, beat together the butter, honey, and cayenne on high speed until very light and fluffy. Serve alongside the cornbread.

PUMPKIN SPICE BREAD

This is one of the most popular autumn treats at the bake shop. The smell of cinnamon, ginger, and cloves along with the pumpkin draws in passersby off the street. Don't let the number of spices in this recipe intimidate you; you likely already have many of them in your spice drawer! I promise it will be worth it when you taste the complex and carefully balanced flavors. This bread freezes very well: simply wrap in plastic wrap or store in an airtight container.

1 cup / 227 g butter, room temperature

2 cups packed / 488 g golden brown sugar

3 eggs

1 (15-ounce) can / 425 g pumpkin puree

1 cup / 190 g potato starch

1 cup / 130 g tapioca starch

1 cup / 170 g white rice flour

2 teaspoons / 10 g baking powder

1 teaspoon / 4.6 g baking soda

$^1/_2$ teaspoon / 2.4 g sea salt

$^3/_4$ teaspoon / .8 g xanthan gum

1 tablespoon plus 1 teaspoon / 10.4 g cinnamon

1 tablespoon / 5.1 g ground ginger

1 teaspoon / 2.1 g ground cloves

$^1/_2$ teaspoon / 1 g ground allspice

$^1/_2$ cup / 113 g milk

Preheat the oven to 325°F. Spray two 1-pound loaf pans with gluten-free cooking spray and set aside.

Using a stand mixer with a paddle attachment, cream the butter on medium-high speed until light in color, about 5 minutes. Add the sugar and beat until the mixture is light and fluffy. Add the eggs, one at a time, and blend thoroughly, stopping occasionally to scrape down the sides of the bowl. Add the pumpkin puree and beat on low speed until combined. In a separate bowl, combine the starches, rice flour, baking powder, baking soda, salt, xanthan gum, cinnamon, ginger, cloves, and allspice. Add the dry ingredients to the pumpkin-butter mixture in 3 separate additions, alternating with the milk, and blend thoroughly after each addition.

Divide the batter evenly between the two loaf pans and bake until a toothpick inserted in the center comes out clean, 55 to 60 minutes. Let cool completely. Turn out of the pans and slice. Store at room temperature in an airtight container for up to 3 days. The flavors will improve the next day!

LEMON POUND CAKE

{EASY}   Makes 16 thick slices

When I was in college, before I went gluten-free, my friends and I would make it a point to get together for monthly dinners. I don't remember any of the entrées we made, but I do remember that Alison Clode's dessert specialty was a variation of this lemon cake, soaked with a puckery-sweet lemon glaze. It's very quick and easy to make and is a fantastic reason to take a study break.

2³/₄ cups / 625 g sugar

1 cup / 227 g butter, room temperature

¹/₄ cup / 42 g lemon zest

6 large eggs

1 cup / 190 g potato starch

1 cup / 130 g tapioca starch

1 cup / 170 g rice flour

1 teaspoon / 4.6 g baking soda

1 teaspoon / 5 g baking powder

¹/₂ teaspoon / .5 g xanthan gum

¹/₂ teaspoon / 2.4 g salt

1 cup / 244 g sour cream

¹/₂ cup / 113 g fresh-squeezed lemon juice (about 2 large lemons)

LEMON GLAZE

4 cups / 568 g powdered sugar

¹/₂ cup / 113 g fresh-squeezed lemon juice (about 2 large lemons)

Preheat the oven to 350°F. Spray two 1-pound loaf pans with gluten-free cooking spray. Sprinkle ¹/₄ cup of the sugar into one of the pans and tilt the pan to all angles so the sugar covers the bottom and sides of the pan. Pour the loose sugar into the remaining loaf pan and repeat the procedure. Discard any excess sugar.

Using a stand mixer with a paddle attachment, beat the butter until it is light and fluffy and pale in color. Add the remaining 2¹/₂ cups sugar and the lemon zest and beat until once again light and fluffy. Add the eggs, one at a time, and blend thoroughly, stopping occasionally to scrape down the sides of the bowl. In a separate bowl, combine the starches, rice flour, baking soda, baking powder, xanthan gum, and salt. Add a third of the dry ingredients to the butter mixture and blend on low speed. Mix in the sour cream and then add half of the remaining dry ingredients and combine well. Add the lemon juice and the remaining dry ingredients and stir by hand just to blend.

Divide the batter evenly between the two loaf pans. Bake until golden brown and a toothpick inserted in the center just comes out clean, 30 to 35 minutes. Cool the cakes in the pans for about an hour and then invert the cakes onto a parchment-lined baking sheet.

To make the glaze, whisk together the confectioners' sugar and lemon juice until smooth and thick. Pour the lemon glaze over the top of the cakes. Let set for about an hour. Then slice and enjoy!

BEER BREAD

When I was in elementary school, my mom worked at the hospital near our house. Because she left for work at 5:30 and the school bus didn't come until 7:15, the next-door neighbors, Sylvia and Jim, often watched me in the mornings. Jim was a home brewer and baker and often combined the two with his own homemade beer bread. I loved showing up next door, still sleepy-eyed and groggy, and letting the sweet smell of freshly baked bread wash over me as I awakened. Jim's secret was buttering his bread as it came out of the oven. If you want to do the same, simply melt ¼ cup of butter and drizzle it over the bread as soon as it's finished baking. If you're dairy-free, use coconut butter instead or sprinkle an extra ½ teaspoon of salt over the batter before it bakes. Use as pale an ale as you can find: dark gluten-free beers tend to give the bread a bitter flavor. I really like New Grist Gluten-Free Sorghum and Rice beer.

1 cup / 130 g tapioca starch

3/4 cup / 142 g potato starch

3/4 cup / 110 g millet flour

¼ cup / 40 g sweet white rice flour

⅓ cup packed / 71 g brown sugar

1 tablespoon / 14 g baking powder

1 teaspoon / 4.7 g salt

½ teaspoon / .5 g xanthan gum

1 (12-ounce) bottle or can / 340 ml pale gluten-free beer or dry English cider, unopened and at room temperature

½ cup / 113 g butter, melted

½ teaspoon / 1.8 g coarse kosher salt

Preheat the oven to 350°F. Spray a large (2-pound) loaf pan with gluten-free cooking spray and line with parchment paper.

In a large bowl, combine the starches, flours, sugar, baking powder, salt, and xanthan gum. Make a well in the center of the dry ingredients and pour in the beer and the butter. Mix to moisten the dry ingredients.

Pour the batter into the loaf pan and spread evenly. Sprinkle with the coarse salt and bake until a toothpick inserted in the center comes out clean, 50 to 55 minutes. Let cool completely before turning out of the pan and slicing.

Cookies, Brownies, and Bar Treats

CHILDHOOD REVISITED

When I was in elementary school, my favorite part of school lunch was (surprise!) dessert. I loved opening up my She-Ra lunch box and finding what dessert was stashed beneath the love note from my mom and my squished PBJ sandwich. Sometimes it was a couple of store-bought chocolate chip cookies, but on occasion I was lucky enough to get homemade brownies or crispy rice treats, making me the center of envy at my lunch table.

Children (many in very grown-up bodies) love the treats presented in this chapter. Include any one of these in their lunch and you'll be pretty much assured they'll have the best dessert among their friends!

MOCHA TRUFFLE FUDGE BROWNIES

Like most children, I loved it when my mom would bake something sweet: it didn't much matter what it was, as long as I could lick the bowl and spoon. One of her specialties was a dense mocha fudge cake with espresso chocolate icing. These fudgy little bites are modeled on that theme. If you're sensitive to caffeine, try decaf espresso powder. You can substitute very strong coffee for the espresso if you prefer.

1³/₄ cups / 397 g granulated sugar

1 cup / 99 g unsweetened cocoa powder

¹/₄ cup / 47 g potato starch

¹/₄ cup / 31 g tapioca starch

1 teaspoon / 4.7 g salt

2 eggs

¹/₃ cup / 74 g canola oil

2 tablespoons / 10 g instant espresso powder dissolved in ¹/₄ cup water

1 tablespoon / 14 g vanilla extract

MOCHA FROSTING

6 tablespoons / 28 g unsweetened cocoa powder

¹/₄ cup / 51 g shortening

2 cups / 284 g confectioners' sugar

¹/₂ cup / 113 g strong coffee, cooled

¹/₂ teaspoon / 2.5 g vanilla extract

Preheat the oven to 350°F. Spray an 8-inch square baking pan with gluten-free cooking spray and line with parchment paper so the ends extend over the top of the pan. Lightly spray the parchment paper.

In a large bowl, combine the sugar, cocoa powder, starches, and salt. Whisk in the eggs, oil, espresso, and vanilla until well combined.

Pour the batter into the baking pan and bake until a toothpick inserted in the center comes out clean, 40 to 45 minutes. Let the brownies cool completely and then refrigerate in the pan for 1 hour.

To make the frosting, place the cocoa powder and shortening in a mixing bowl and, using a stand mixer with a paddle attachment, beat on low speed until combined. Then beat on high until creamy and several shades lighter. Blend in the confectioners' sugar, 1 cup at a time, and slowly drizzle in the coffee and vanilla until well combined. Turn the mixer to high to ensure a uniform consistency.

Spread the frosting evenly over the brownies. Using the ends of the parchment paper, lift the brownies out of the pan and cut into squares.

GINGER MOLASSES COOKIES

{EASY}   Makes 4 dozen cookies

My first memory of ginger molasses cookies was from Halloween the year I was ten. Our class had a Halloween party at Kent's house, and his mother made ginger molasses cookies, rolled in sugar before baking to give them a sparkling sheen. I loved the soft, chewy cookies, eating way more than my fair share. Most ginger molasses cookies I've eaten since have fallen short of the memory, but *these* cookies are spicy and chewy and crisp around the edges all at once. They make fantastic treats for school lunches and can be frozen either before or after they're baked for up to 2 weeks. If you have any left over, you can use them as the crust for Mascarpone Cheesecake (page 114) or S'Mores Tartlets (page 50).

1½ cups / 340 g butter

3 cups / 681 g granulated sugar

1 cup packed / 244 g dark
    brown sugar

1 cup / 329 g molasses

4 eggs

2 cups / 340 g sweet white rice flour

2 cups / 260 g tapioca starch

2 cups / 380 g potato starch

1½ cups / 221 g millet flour

½ cup / 78 g cornstarch

1 tablespoon plus 1½ teaspoons /
    20.8 g baking soda

2 teaspoons / 2 g xanthan gum

1 teaspoon / 4.7 g salt

1 tablespoon plus 1 teaspoon /
    6.8 g ground ginger

2½ teaspoons / 6.5 g cinnamon

2½ teaspoons / 5.3 g cloves

Using a stand mixer with a paddle attachment, cream the butter, 2 cups of the granulated sugar, the brown sugar, and the molasses on high speed until very light and fluffy. Don't rush this step: it may take 5 minutes or more. Add the eggs, one at a time, and blend thoroughly, stopping occasionally to scrape down the sides of the bowl. In a large bowl, combine the flours, starches, cornstarch, baking soda, xanthan gum, salt, ginger, cinnamon, and cloves. Add the dry ingredients to the butter mixture in 3 additions, mixing on low speed after each addition. Chill until cool and firm, about an hour.

Preheat the oven to 300°F. Line several baking sheets with parchment paper.

Scoop the dough into golf ball–sized scoops and roll in the remaining cup of granulated sugar. Place the dough balls on the baking sheets 3 inches apart. Bake until set to the touch and lightly golden brown, 12 to 15 minutes. If using multiple baking sheets at once, bake for 6 minutes, then rotate and continue baking until the cookies are done.

CHILE LIME COCONUT MACAROONS

{EASY}   Makes about 21 cookies

I first met Brandy, aka Mrs. Alaska 2011, at the Gluten & Allergen Free Expo in Chicago. She was the emcee for a baking seminar I was teaching and, as a nurse practitioner with celiac disease, she was excited and knowledgeable about gluten-free lifestyles. When I found out that she missed her hometown of Atlanta, I started thinking about desserts I could make to give her a taste of home. They like things hot in Atlanta, so I tweaked my coconut macaroon recipe by adding a little cayenne and the citrusy tang of lime zest for some of the sweet heat that she was missing in Anchorage. Be sure to bake these until they are dark golden brown on top: they'll still be moist and chewy inside, but the longer baking time ensures a crunchy counterpoint. If you don't want the spicy kick, leave out the cayenne.

4³/₄ cups / 537 g desiccated macaroon coconut (not sweet-ened flaked coconut)

2 cups / 454 g sugar

1 tablespoon plus 1¹/₂ teaspoons / 10.5 g coconut flour

1 tablespoon / 10.5 g freshly grated lime zest

³/₄ teaspoon / 1.3 g cayenne pepper

¹/₂ teaspoon / 2.4 g salt

1 cup / 272 g egg whites (from about 8 large eggs)

3 tablespoons / 58 g honey

1 teaspoon / 5 g vanilla extract

Preheat the oven to 350°F. Line two large baking sheets with parchment paper and set aside.

In a large bowl, combine the coconut, sugar, coconut flour, lime zest, cayenne, and salt. In a separate bowl, mix together the egg whites, honey, and vanilla. Make a well in the coconut mixture and pour the egg white mix into the center of the well. Stir together until thoroughly mixed.

Drop golf ball–sized scoops of the coconut mixture close together onto the baking sheets. Bake until dark golden brown and set to the touch, 22 to 28 minutes. Let cool completely on the baking sheet, then peel off of the parchment and store in an airtight container. You can make the "dough" ahead of time and freeze unbaked on the baking sheet for up to 2 weeks or freeze in an airtight container once they've been baked for a month (if they last that long).

S'MORES TARTLETS

{INTERMEDIATE}   Makes 3 dozen tartlets

When I was a kid, my favorite part of camp was the cookout. While hot dogs were carefully distributed (one per camper), a cabin of eight kids and two counselors was often given two full bags of marshmallows, a box of graham crackers, and five large chocolate bars. Once the sun went down, our counselors would build the campfire and we would line up to receive our hot dog, potato chips, and carrot sticks. But it was the S'Mores that we were *really* excited about.

I never much liked graham crackers, so this twist on basic S'Mores appeals more to my grown-up tastes. These are best eaten the day they are assembled; however, you can make and bake the ginger cookie crust and chocolate ganache filling and store in airtight containers in the freezer up to 2 weeks or refrigerator up to 5 days in advance. Wait to mix the marshmallow Italian meringue until just before you're ready to serve.

GINGER COOKIE CRUST

$2^1/_4$ cups ground cookie crumbs (from about 10 Ginger Molasses Cookies if you use the recipe on page 46, or about 14 ounces of spicy gingersnap cookies if using store-bought)

$^1/_3$ cup / 71 g butter, melted

CHOCOLATE GANACHE FILLING

2 cups / 352 g good-quality dark chocolate

2 cups / 476 ml heavy cream

2 eggs

MARSHMALLOW MERINGUE

$^1/_4$ cup / 57 g sugar

2 tablespoons / 28 ml water

$^1/_4$ cup / 68 g egg whites (from about 2 large eggs)

$^1/_8$ teaspoon cream of tartar

$^1/_2$ teaspoon / 3.8 g vanilla extract

Preheat the oven to 350°F. Line two 24-cup mini muffin pans with 36 mini liners and set aside.

Crush the cookies in the bowl of a food processor or in a double-lined plastic bag using a rolling pin. Put the crumbs in a bowl and stir in the butter to combine. Divide the crumbs among the muffin cups (about $1^1/_2$ tablespoons in each). Gently press down to cover the bottoms. Bake until firm and bubbly, 10 to 14 minutes. Remove from the oven and decrease the temperature to 325°F.

Place the chocolate in a heatproof bowl. Gently scald the cream in a saucepan over medium heat until it is steaming and small bubbles form just at the edge, about 4 minutes. Pour the cream over the chocolate and let stand for a moment, then stir to combine. In a separate bowl, beat the eggs well. Slowly add small amounts of the chocolate mixture (about $^1/_4$ cup at a time) to the eggs in 3 additions, whisking vigorously after each addition. Then add the egg mixture back into the remaining chocolate-cream mixture.

Fill the muffin cups almost to the top and bake until bubbly and just set, 12 to 15 minutes: gentle shaking should cause the chocolate mixture to jiggle slightly in the center but

continued

not look liquid. Remove from the oven and let cool to room temperature, about 45 minutes. Chill until ready to serve.

To make the meringue, stir together the sugar and water in a small saucepan. Wipe down the sides of the pan with a wet pastry brush to ensure that no sugar crystals get in the syrup. Heat until boiling and a candy thermometer reaches 248°F, about 12 minutes.

Meanwhile, using a stand mixer with a whip attachment, whip the egg whites and cream of tartar on medium-high until soft peaks form and mixture looks thick and foamy and white with tiny bubbles. Turn to medium-low and very slowly pour in the hot sugar syrup. Turn to high and whip until very thick and glossy and the bowl is starting to cool, about 7 minutes. Blend in the vanilla.

Dollop a tablespoon or two of the meringue on top of each tartlet and either broil for 1 to 2 minutes or use a kitchen torch to gently brown the meringue. Eat within 4 hours.

LINZER BARS

My mother-in-law, Brigitte, is German and a fantastic baker. Each year for Christmas, she rolls up her sleeves, dusts off her ancient nut grinder, and spends four entire days producing almond flour–based cookies. One of my husband's favorites is the Linzer cookie. This gluten-free version, in bar form, takes far less time to make. Besides the great flavor, the best thing about these bars is that the almond base is not overly sweet. While my mother-in-law makes her own jam, I've tried many kinds of store-bought jams with great results.

1 cup / 227 g butter, room temperature

²/₃ cup / 151 g sugar

1 large / 20 g egg yolk

1 teaspoon / 5 g vanilla extract

2 tablespoons / 21 g orange zest

1 cup / 110 g powdered almonds, or 1¹/₂ cups whole almonds, finely ground

³/₄ cup / 110 g millet flour

³/₄ cup / 122 g sweet white rice flour

¹/₂ cup / 67 g tapioca starch, plus extra for rolling out dough

1 teaspoon / 1 g xanthan gum

¹/₂ teaspoon / 1.3 g cinnamon

¹/₄ teaspoon / 1.2 g salt

³/₄ cup / 255 g raspberry or apricot preserves

¹/₃ cup / 50 g confectioners' sugar

Preheat the oven to 325°F. Spray a 9 by 11-inch baking pan with gluten-free cooking spray and line with parchment paper.

Using a stand mixer with a paddle attachment, cream the butter on high speed until light and fluffy. Add the sugar and continue beating until pale in color and very fluffy. Blend in the egg yolk, vanilla, and orange zest, stopping to scrape down the sides of the bowl. In a small bowl, combine the almonds, flours, tapioca starch, xanthan gum, cinnamon, and salt. Add the dry ingredients to the butter mixture and combine on low speed.

Press two-thirds of the dough into the bottom of the baking pan. Chill until firm, about an hour. Then spread the raspberry preserves evenly across the dough. Roll out the remaining third of the dough to ¹/₄ inch thick, using tapioca starch to prevent it from sticking. With a knife, pizza cutter, or fluted pastry roller, cut even strips of dough about ¹/₄ to ¹/₂ inch wide. Gently arrange strips of dough on the diagonal, about ¹/₂ inch apart. Lay the remaining strips vertically, ¹/₂ inch apart, to create a lattice pattern.

Bake until the dough is lightly golden brown, 25 to 35 minutes. Let cool completely. Then gently sift the confectioners' sugar over the top and cut into bars about 1¹/₂ inches wide by 3 inches long.

LEMON-GLAZED MADELEINES

{INTERMEDIATE}   Makes 24 madeleines

I first met Sheila when she came into the bakery during opening weekend. She bit into a lemon madeleine and immediately teared up. I came around the counter and asked if she was okay. She grinned at me through her tears and said, "I'm just so thrilled that you're here. I have been celiac for seven years and in all that time haven't tasted anything this delicious." She is now a regular customer, friend, and taste-tester for me. Whenever I'm developing new recipes, I know I've struck gold when Sheila tears up.

3 tablespoons / 47 g butter, melted

1/2 cup / 113 g sugar

2 eggs

2 tablespoons / 21 g lemon zest (from about 1 large lemon)

1/2 cup / 113 g butter, melted and slightly cooled

1/2 cup / 67 g tapioca starch

1/2 cup / 95 g potato starch

LEMON GLAZE

1 cup / 142 g confectioners' sugar

3 tablespoons / 47 g lemon juice

Generously brush a madeleine pan with the 3 tablespoons of butter, reserving any unused portion for later.

In a stand mixer with a whisk attachment, whip the sugar and eggs on high speed until thick, light, and foamy and the mixture reaches the "ribbon stage": if you drip a spoonful of the mixture across the surface, it forms a ribbon, visible for 3 seconds before it sinks back into the mixture. This may take a while and should not be rushed. Blend in the lemon zest and the 1/2 cup of butter until combined. Then fold in the starches.

Fill a pastry bag with the batter (or use a zip-top bag with a corner snipped off) and let stand in the refrigerator for 30 to 60 minutes.

Preheat the oven to 400°F.

Pipe the batter into the madeleine pan, filling about two-thirds full. Bake until lightly golden brown and a toothpick inserted in the madeleine comes out clean, 6 to 9 minutes. Immediately after baking, turn the madeleines out of the pan onto parchment paper. Let cool completely. If you are baking in batches, keep any remaining batter chilled between each batch. If needed, brush the pans with the reserved butter and fill with batter and bake.

Stir together the confectioners' sugar and lemon juice until the mixture is smooth and lump-free. Consistency will be fairly thin. Use additional lemon juice to thin out the glaze as needed. Dip the shell pattern of each madeleine into the glaze and place glaze side up on a baking sheet or serving plate. Let the glaze set about 30 to 60 minutes, then serve and enjoy!

ALMOND BISCOTTI

{EASY}   Makes about 24 biscotti

Upon graduating from pastry school, I worked at clarklewis restaurant in downtown Portland. It had a funky stainless silver espresso machine, and we always served a biscotto with each espresso drink, sometimes turning out several dozen each night. This recipe is loosely based on the one I used at the restaurant and is delicious with or without an espresso to dunk it in. The anise seed, orange zest, and almonds combine to lend a classic flavor, reminiscent of what you might eat at a small café in Verona.

3/4 cup / 170 g sugar

3/4 cup / 122 g sweet white rice flour

1/2 cup / 74 g millet flour

1/2 cup / 67 g tapioca starch

2 teaspoons / 2 g xanthan gum

1 teaspoon / 5 g baking powder

1/4 teaspoon / 1.2 g salt

4 eggs

2 teaspoons / 7 g orange zest

2 teaspoons / 5 g anise seeds

2/3 cup / 57 g blanched almonds

Preheat the oven to 350°F. Line a baking sheet with parchment paper and set aside.

In a mixing bowl, combine the sugar, flours, tapioca starch, xanthan gum, baking powder, and salt. Add the eggs one at a time and blend thoroughly. Stir in the orange zest and the anise seeds to distribute throughout, then mix in the almonds. The dough will be slightly sticky.

Pat the dough into a log the length of the baking sheet and smooth the top. Bake until the log is set and golden brown and a toothpick inserted in the center comes out clean, 22 to 26 minutes. If you gently squeeze the sides, there should be resistance and the dough should feel like it has a crust on it. Let sit to cool slightly, about 6 minutes. With a serrated knife, cut the log on a slight diagonal into slices 1/2 inch thick. Arrange the slices on the baking sheet broad side up and bake until the cookies feel dry and set, 8 to 12 minutes longer. Remove from the oven and let cool completely.

These are delicious when stored at room temperature in an airtight container and will keep for a week or so. If you'd like to freeze them, do so; it will extend the shelf life substantially.

PEANUT BUTTER TRUFFLE CRISPY RICE BARS

{EASY}   Makes 18 bars

When I was thirteen, my friend Christina and I made crispy rice bars after school, intending to sell them to classmates the next day. We painstakingly melted the butter, stirred in the marshmallows and vanilla, and struggled with the crispy rice cereal. After waiting patiently for the bars to set up, we decided to cut just a teeny tiny corner to taste, for quality control. That was our downfall. Before we knew it, we had consumed more than half the pan! This recipe is a fantastic spin on that old-fashioned dessert, and it looks much fancier and more time consuming than it actually is. Most of the time involved is just waiting for the various layers to chill enough to add the next element. The browned butter is a simple step that elevates the entire flavor of the crispy rice layer.

CRISPY RICE LAYER

1/4 cup / 57 g butter

1 (10-ounce) bag / 283 g jumbo
  marshmallows (I like Kraft
  Jet-Puffed)

2 teaspoons / 10 g vanilla extract

8 cups / 283 g gluten-free crispy rice
  cereal (such as Erewhon)

PEANUT BUTTER LAYER

2 cups / 284 g confectioners' sugar,
  sifted

1 cup / 269 g creamy peanut butter

1/2 cup / 113 g butter

1 teaspoon / 5 g vanilla extract

CHOCOLATE LAYER

2 cups / 352 g dark chocolate

1/4 cup / 57 g butter

Spray an 8 by 11-inch baking pan with gluten-free cooking spray and set aside.

To make the crispy rice layer, melt the butter in a large pot over medium heat, stirring occasionally, until the butter browns, 3 to 5 minutes. Add the marshmallows and vanilla and stir continuously until the marshmallows are melted. Remove from heat and stir in the cereal. Pour entire contents into the baking pan. Wet or grease your hands and pat down the cereal so it is level and compact. Freeze for 15 minutes to cool and set.

Using a stand mixer with a paddle attachment, combine all the ingredients for the peanut butter layer and blend on low speed. Remove the crispy rice layer from the freezer and spread the peanut butter filling evenly over it. Freeze until firm to the touch, 30 to 60 minutes.

In a microwave-safe bowl, or over a double boiler, melt the chocolate and butter for the chocolate layer and stir together until smooth. If using the microwave, heat at 30-second intervals, stirring well in between each interval. Working quickly, spread the chocolate evenly over the peanut butter layer. If the peanut butter is cold, the chocolate will set quickly.

Freeze the pan again, 15 to 30 minutes, as it will be much easier to cut if the peanut butter layer is firm. Cut into bars and serve cold or at room temperature.

SPICED APPLE CRUMB BARS

{EASY}   Makes 12 bars

Skip the turkey and gravy: my favorite Thanksgiving food has always been apple pie. Long before I hit upon a winning combination for flaky, gluten-free piecrust that tasted like "real" crust, I developed a brown sugar shortbread that makes the fantastic base for these Spiced Apple Crumb Bars. Even though it isn't pie, and even though it might not be Thanksgiving, you'll still give thanks for these delicious treats.

SHORTBREAD BASE

1 cup / 227 g butter

1 cup packed / 244 g brown sugar

1 cup / 147 g millet flour

1 cup / 170 g sweet white rice flour

1 cup / 130 g tapioca starch

1/2 teaspoon / 2.4 g salt

FILLING

8 whole / 1.4 kg tart green apples
   (I prefer Granny Smith)

1 1/3 cups packed / 315 g brown sugar

1/4 cup / 31 g tapioca starch

2 teaspoons / 5.2 g cinnamon

1/2 teaspoon / .9 g ground ginger

1/4 teaspoon / .5 g ground nutmeg

1/4 teaspoon / .5 g ground cardamom

1/4 teaspoon / .5 g ground cloves

1/4 teaspoon / 1.2 g salt

1 1/2 teaspoons / 7 g lemon juice

1 teaspoon / 5 g vanilla extract

Preheat the oven to 325°F. Spray a 13 by 9-inch baking pan with gluten-free cooking spray and line with parchment paper.

To make the base, using a stand mixer with a paddle attachment, cream the butter on high speed until light and creamy. Add the brown sugar and beat until fluffy and several shades lighter. In a small bowl, combine the flours, tapioca starch, and salt. Blend half the flour mixture into the butter mixture on low speed, stopping occasionally to scrape down the sides of the bowl. Add the remaining flour mixture and repeat the process.

Press two-thirds of the mixture into the baking pan, reserving the remaining third. Bake until lightly golden brown and set to the touch, about 40 minutes.

To make the filling, peel and core the apples, dice into quarter-inch cubes, and place in a large pot. You can immerse the apples in water while you're peeling and cutting to prevent them from turning brown. Simply drain off the water when you're finished. Stir in the brown sugar, tapioca starch, cinnamon, ginger, nutmeg, cardamom, cloves, salt, lemon juice, and vanilla. Heat over medium-low heat, stirring occasionally, until the apples start to caramelize, 10 to 15 minutes.

Spread the apples over the shortbread base and crumble the remaining dough over the apples. Bake until the cookie top is lightly golden and set, 15 to 20 minutes. Let cool completely before cutting. Serve alone or with a scoop of your favorite vanilla ice cream.

OATMEAL CHOCOLATE-CHIP COOKIES

{EASY}   Makes 20 large cookies

My grandfather was a pharmacist for Thrifty Drugstore in Southern California. Besides the usual items, Thrifty was known for 25-cent ice cream cones, with lots of different flavors. I loved when we could take a stroll the eight blocks to Papa's work, pick up a couple of chocolate chip ice cream cones and a bag of oatmeal raisin cookies, and walk back to the house, trying to keep the ice cream from dripping all over the pavement. I loved the spiced cookies with the cold ice cream but was not a fan of the raisins. This recipe is derived from a family favorite for oatmeal raisin cookies, but I've replaced the raisins with chocolate chips so you don't have to fling them away!

$^1/_2$ cup / 113 g butter, room temperature

$^1/_2$ cup / 113 g granulated sugar

$^3/_4$ cup packed / 190 g golden brown sugar

1 teaspoon / 5 g vanilla extract

2 large eggs

1 cup / 92 g gluten-free oats

$^1/_2$ cup / 74 g millet flour

$^1/_2$ cup / 95 g potato starch

$^1/_2$ cup / 67 g tapioca starch

1 teaspoon / 1 g xanthan gum

1 teaspoon / 4.6 g baking soda

1 teaspoon / 4.7 g salt

$^1/_2$ teaspoon / 1.3 g ground cinnamon

$^1/_4$ teaspoon / .5 g ground nutmeg

$^1/_8$ teaspoon / .3 g ground cloves

1 (11-ounce) bag (about 1$^3/_4$ cups / 312 g) semisweet chocolate chips

Preheat the oven to 350°F. Line 2 baking sheets with parchment paper and set aside.

Using a stand mixer with a paddle attachment, cream the butter on high speed until very light and fluffy. This may take 5 to 10 minutes, depending on how cool your butter is. Add the sugars and beat until well combined, stopping occasionally to scrape down the sides of the bowl. On medium speed, mix in the vanilla and eggs. In a separate bowl, combine the oats, millet flour, starches, xanthan gum, baking soda, salt, cinnamon, nutmeg, and cloves. Add the dry ingredients to the butter mixture in 3 additions, blending thoroughly after each addition. Stir in the chocolate chips by hand.

Drop golf ball–sized scoops of the dough onto the baking sheets 3 inches apart. Bake until the edges are golden brown and the centers are soft but set, 10 to 14 minutes. Let cool on the baking sheets a few minutes to set, then remove to a cooling rack or a brown paper bag, cut open (my preference because it soaks up extra grease). Freeze anything you don't plan to eat within a week.

Puddings, Cakes, and Other Pastries

COMFORT AND AMAZE!

The summer after I graduated from college found me backpacking through Europe. After a quick trip to Paris, I bought a Eurail pass and headed over the mountains to Chamonix-Mont-Blanc. I stayed at the Red Mountain Lodge, the quintessential ski chalet, which sat at the top of the cobblestone road that wound through the village. Private accommodations were negligibly more expensive than a dorm room in the town's hostel, and the price included breakfast, which depended on the whim of the chef: some mornings it was croissants, Nutella, and jam and other mornings yogurt, flapjacks, or coconut-ginger oatmeal.

Between the setting, the food, and the people I met, I had such a wonderful time in Chamonix that I ended up staying there five of my eight weeks in Europe. The lodge chef, Michael Brown, was an award-winning Aussie drawn to Chamonix because of the snowboarding and extreme mountain biking. And he made the single best cake I've ever tasted.

Jess, one of the Canadian lodgers, was turning twenty-four, and Michael decided to make something special for her birthday. With me acting as sous-chef, Michael whipped up a deep, dark chocolate torte with fresh pineapple puree and candied rose petals. While no chocolate cake I've tasted since has compared to Jess's birthday cake, I am still transported to that time whenever I make a gluten-free dark chocolate cake. It was there the seeds of inspiration to become a pastry chef really germinated, to make fabulous desserts that would make others feel as special as Michael made Jess feel on her birthday.

BUBBIE'S SECRET HONEY CAKE

{EASY}   Makes 16 servings (or 4 servings, if one of those people is my dad)

My great-grandmother Bubbie was known for her moist, rich, honey cake, but she carefully guarded the recipe. Years after Bubbie had passed away, when I was visiting my grandmother, I asked for a copy of the recipe, but the one I got didn't contain honey! The night before I left, around 3 a.m., I tiptoed into the pantry and secretly copied the recipe from the family cookbook. When I got home and made the honey cake according to the recipe, it wasn't nearly as good as the version Bubbie made. Not satisfied, I began tinkering with the ingredients and came up with something that tastes very similar to the original. I've since adapted my version to be gluten-free. My dad always requests that I slightly underbake the cake so the top remains extra moist and delicious! Bubbie's original recipe contained rye whiskey, but I've since switched to bourbon. Look for one labeled "Kentucky straight bourbon."

1¹/₃ cups / 484 g honey

1 cup / 227 ml very strong hot coffee or espresso

1³/₄ cups / 397 g sugar

1 cup / 218 g canola oil

4 large eggs, beaten

1 cup / 130 g tapioca starch

1 cup / 190 g potato starch

1 cup / 170 g rice flour

2 teaspoons / 10 g baking powder

1 teaspoon / 4.6 g baking soda

1 teaspoon / 4.7 g salt

2 tablespoons / 28.3 g bourbon

Preheat the oven to 300°F. Spray a 9 by 13-inch baking pan with gluten-free cooking spray and set aside.

In a large heatproof bowl, stir together the honey and hot coffee. In a separate bowl, mix together the sugar, oil, and eggs until smooth. In another bowl, combine the starches, rice flour, baking powder, baking soda, and salt. Pour the honey mixture into the oil mixture and whisk to blend well. Add this mixture to the dry ingredients and stir gently, just until combined. Gently stir in the bourbon.

Pour the batter into the baking pan. Give the pan a few knocks on the counter to prevent tunneling and bake until a toothpick inserted in the center comes out clean, 55 to 60 minutes. The top should still be rather soft and almost gooey, which is the very best part of this cake! Let cool completely, cut into squares, and enjoy with a cup of strong coffee.

CHOCOLATE MOUSSE MERINGUE PIE

{INTERMEDIATE}   Makes 10 servings

My mom's birthday falls near Thanksgiving, so when she was a little girl, it was often jointly celebrated with that holiday. Because of this, my mom often had to eat foods she didn't much care for on her birthday: turkey, gravy, and green beans. Her one request—which she always received—was a chocolate mousse pie for dessert. Naturally, this is one of the first gluten-free recipes I developed.

MERINGUE CRUST

¹/₂ cup / 136 g egg whites (from about 4 large eggs)

¹/₄ teaspoon cream of tartar

1¹/₂ cups / 340 g sugar

1 teaspoon / 5 g vanilla extract

MOUSSE FILLING

1¹/₄ cups / 221 g dark or semisweet chocolate chips (not unsweetened)

1 whole egg

2 egg yolks

1 teaspoon / 5 g rum or vanilla extract

2 egg whites

1¹/₂ cups / 357 g heavy whipping cream

Chocolate shavings (optional)

Preheat the oven to 200°F. Spray a 9-inch deep-dish pie pan with gluten-free cooking spray and set aside.

To make the meringue crust, put the egg whites and cream of tartar in a clean, dry mixing bowl. Using a stand mixer with a whip attachment, beat on high speed until thick and fluffy and medium peaks hold. On medium speed, slowly add the sugar, then turn to high. Beat mixture to glossy, firm peaks. Mix in the vanilla.

Spread into the pie pan and bake until the meringue is crisp and firm to the touch if you tap it, about 2 hours. Cool completely before filling.

To make the mousse, melt the chocolate in a double boiler over hot water. Whisk the egg and egg yolks into the chocolate one at a time. Stir in the rum. In a clean, dry mixing bowl, beat the egg whites to medium-stiff peaks. Gently fold into the chocolate mixture. Using the same mixing bowl, beat 1 cup of the cream until medium peaks form. Fold gently into the chocolate mixture in 3 additions, each after the previous one is about 90 percent incorporated.

Spoon the chocolate mousse into the meringue and chill for 4 hours or overnight. To serve, beat the remaining ¹/₂ cup of cream and garnish the top of the pie with the whipped cream and chocolate shavings.

COCONUT RICE PUDDING

{EASY}   Makes 8 servings

When I was growing up, there was this great little Indian restaurant not too far from our house that had eight tables and a long wait. I always made sure to save room for multiple servings of the "kheer" rice pudding, which was studded with cardamom, cloves, and slivered almonds. This version incorporates the cardamom and rose water from the original but not the almonds. If you want to add some, you're welcome to do so! I developed this recipe for a dinner guest who was egg- and dairy-intolerant. But because the coconut milk was such a delightful flavor addition, I've never gone back. If you don't mind that the mixture thickens as it cools, you can make this ahead of time and store it in the refrigerator for several days. It makes a fantastic breakfast on hot summer mornings!

5 cups / 1133 ml water

2 cups / 400 g jasmine rice

3/4 cup / 170 g sugar

1/2 teaspoon / 1 g ground cardamom

1/2 teaspoon / 1.3 g cinnamon

2 tablespoons / 28.3 g rose water

1 teaspoon / 5 g vanilla extract

1 (13.5-ounce) can / 382 g coconut milk

Put the water in a saucepan on high heat to boil.

Meanwhile, put the rice in a strainer or a sieve lined with a tea towel and rinse under cold running water until the water runs clear and most of the starch has been rinsed away, 5 to 10 minutes.

Once the water has come to a boil, stir in the sugar, cardamom, cinnamon, rose water, and vanilla and then the rice. Cover and turn the heat to low. Simmer for 15 to 20 minutes, stirring occasionally, until the water is mostly absorbed. Add the coconut milk and simmer, stirring occasionally, until the mixture looks thick and soupy, about 10 minutes more.

Remove from the heat and serve immediately or let cool and serve chilled.

OATMEAL CAKE

{EASY}   Makes 16 servings

My stepdad, Chuck, has never had much of a sweet tooth. The one exception was his mother's oatmeal cake. When I began experimenting with gluten-free baking, several years after Chuck's mom had passed away, her oatmeal cake was at the top of my to-make list. This moist, slightly spicy cake is good right out of the oven, but even better if you let it sit for a day or two. The vanilla glaze on top adds another layer of gooey goodness.

1 cup / 92 g gluten-free quick oats

1½ cups / 354 ml boiling water

½ cup / 113 g butter

2 cups / 488 g brown sugar

1 teaspoon / 5 g vanilla extract

2 eggs

½ cup / 67 g tapioca starch

½ cup / 95 g potato starch

½ cup / 89 g rice flour

2 teaspoons / 10 g baking powder

1 teaspoon / 4.6 g baking soda

1 teaspoon / 2.6 g cinnamon

½ teaspoon / 2.4 g salt

¼ teaspoon / .3 g xanthan gum

VANILLA GLAZE

2 cups / 284 g confectioners' sugar

¼ cup / 57 g milk

1 teaspoon / 5 g vanilla extract

Preheat the oven to 325°F. Spray either two large (2-pound) loaf pans or one 9 by 13-inch baking pan with gluten-free cooking spray and set aside.

Put the oats in a heatproof container and stir in the boiling water. Then set aside. Using a stand mixer with a paddle attachment, cream the butter until light and fluffy. Beat in the brown sugar until very creamy. Add the vanilla and then the eggs, one at a time, blending thoroughly after each. In a separate bowl, combine the starches, rice flour, baking powder, baking soda, cinnamon, salt, and xanthan gum. Add the dry ingredients to the butter mixture in 3 additions, alternating with the oats, and blend thoroughly after each addition, stopping occasionally to scrape down the sides of the bowl.

Pour the batter into the loaf pans and bake until golden brown and a toothpick inserted in the center comes out clean, 35 to 45 minutes. Let cool completely.

To make the glaze, whisk together the confectioners' sugar, milk, and vanilla until smooth and shiny. Pour liberally over the cake and let set, about an hour. Then slice and serve!

Wrap leftover cake or store in an airtight container at room temperature or in the freezer. You can also make the batter ahead of time and store in the refrigerator for several days: just wrap well or place in an airtight container.

CHOCOLATE-GINGER POTS DE CRÈME

{EASY}   Makes 8 servings

My husband spent the first five years of his life on Kauai, and for as long as I can remember, my family has vacationed there, so it naturally became our go-to vacation spot when we could afford to sneak away. Our most recent trip was deliciously languid, and when we got hungry we walked to Papaya's Natural Foods Market and ate lunch in the grass beneath the coconut palms. I stumbled across a local, organic, dairy-free dark chocolate bar with crystallized ginger and toasted coconut. As soon as we came home, I made this Chocolate-Ginger Pots de Crème to recapture the relaxed, indulgent feeling of the islands.

2 (14-ounce) cans / 793 ml coconut milk

8 egg yolks

1/2 cup / 113 g sugar

3/4 cup / 132 g dark chocolate

2 tablespoons / 45 g crystallized ginger, finely chopped

Preheat the oven to 300°F. Arrange eight 6-ounce ceramic or ovenproof ramekins in a baking dish with sides at least 2 inches high.

Heat the coconut milk over medium heat until steaming. Be careful not to heat too quickly or the milk will scorch the bottom of the pan. Meanwhile, in a stainless steel bowl, whisk together the egg yolks and sugar until smooth. Once the coconut milk is steaming, remove from the heat, add the chocolate, and whisk until the chocolate has melted completely. Slowly pour the milk mixture into the egg mixture, whisking constantly, to allow the milk to gradually bring up the temperature of the yolks so they don't scramble. Once the mixture is smooth, pour it into the ramekins. Sprinkle on the ginger, distributing evenly.

Place the baking dish on the middle rack in the oven. Pour enough water in the pan to come one-half to three-quarters of the way up the outside of the ramekins. Bake until just set, 40 to 50 minutes. If you lightly jiggle the pan, the pots de crème should all move as one (like Jell-O). You can insert the tip of a stainless steel knife into the center to check that it comes out clean or take the internal temperature with a thermometer (which should read 180°F). Cool completely and serve cold or (my preference) cool just a few minutes and serve warm.

HAMANTASCHEN

{INTERMEDIATE}   Makes about 40 cookies

My first experience with hamantaschen was at a holiday cookie exchange hosted by family friends. I slowly circled the cookie-laden table, enthralled with all the different choices. The fruit-filled whole wheat Napoleon hat cookies didn't appeal to me at first, but the tart-sweetness of the apricots and the subtle crunch of the cookie won me over. I later found out that what I had been calling Napoleon hats were, in fact, hamantaschen. Here's my gluten-free, better-than-whole-wheat upgrade. If you don't care for apricots, or would like to shorten the prep time, feel free to substitute your favorite jam in place of the apricot filling. These can be frozen after they're assembled: simply wrap or store in an airtight container for up to 2 weeks, then add 3 or 4 minutes to the baking time.

APRICOT FILLING

1 cup / 170 g dried apricots
(I prefer unsulphered)

$^1/_4$ cup / 57 g sugar

COOKIE DOUGH

$^3/_4$ cup / 96 g tapioca starch, plus
extra for rolling out the dough

$^3/_4$ cup / 122 g sweet white rice flour

$^1/_2$ cup / 74 g millet flour

2 teaspoons / 2 g xanthan gum

Pinch / about .5 g salt

$^1/_2$ cup / 113 g butter, room
temperature

$1^1/_4$ cups / 284 g sugar

2 tablespoons / 28.3 g milk

1 egg

1 teaspoon / 5 g vanilla extract

In a small saucepan, combine the apricots, sugar, and just enough water to mostly cover the apricots (about $1^1/_2$ cups). Cover and heat over medium heat until the water is about to boil. Turn the heat to medium-low and let the apricots simmer for 25 to 30 minutes to absorb the liquid. Remove from the heat and let cool to room temperature, about 20 minutes.

Preheat the oven to 350°F. Line 2 large baking sheets with parchment paper and set aside.

To make the dough, in a small bowl, combine the tapioca starch, flours, xanthan gum, and salt and set aside. Using a stand mixer with a paddle attachment, cream the butter until light and fluffy. Beat in the sugar until the mixture is pale and creamy. Blend in the milk, egg, and vanilla. Add the dry ingredients and mix just until combined. Be careful not to overmix.

Roll out the dough $^1/_4$ inch thick, using the extra tapioca starch to prevent it from sticking. Using a 3-inch biscuit cutter or round cookie cutter, cut the dough into circles and carefully transfer to the baking sheets. Place a teaspoon of apricot filling in the center of each circle. Fold the top quarter of each circle down to partially cover the filling. Rotate the pan slightly more than 90 degrees and fold the top quarter of each circle in partially over the filling. Fold the third side a quarter of the way over the filling and pinch together each point of the triangle of dough so that it resembles a tricorn hat. Bake until golden brown and firm to the touch, 12 to 16 minutes.

CANNOLIZELLI

{INTERMEDIATE}   Makes about 18 cannolizelli

When I was a child, our Christmas Day tradition was making cannoli. My dad grew up in the Bronx and was enamored with Ferraro's Cannoli, a landmark in Little Italy. He had figured out a really great approximation of their recipe, so every year we would carefully stir together the ricotta, confectioners' sugar, spices, and rum, spoon the cannoli filling into the crispy flour tortilla shells, and dust the whole thing with confectioners' sugar. Then we would pile the cannoli on paper plates and deliver them to our friends and neighbors. Nowadays, I make cannoli in a gluten-free shell. Here's how.

SHELLS

3 egg whites

1/2 cup / 113 g sugar

1/3 cup / 71 g butter, melted

1 teaspoon / 5 g vanilla extract

3/4 cup / 122 g sweet white rice flour

1/4 cup / 31 g tapioca starch

1 teaspoon / 5 g baking powder

FILLING

1 (15-ounce) container / 425 g whole milk ricotta cheese

1/2 cup / 71 g confectioners' sugar, plus extra for dusting

1/4 cup / 59 g heavy cream

1 teaspoon / 2.6 g cinnamon

1/4 teaspoon / .9 g freshly grated orange zest

1 1/2 teaspoons / .8 g rum

1/2 teaspoon / 2.5 g vanilla extract

1/4 cup / 43 g semisweet mini chocolate chips

1/4 cup / 31 g toasted pistachio nuts, coarsely chopped (optional)

To make the shells, using a stand mixer with a whip attachment, whip the egg whites and sugar until very thick and pale and fluffy. Then whip in the butter and vanilla. In a small bowl, combine the flour, starch, and baking powder. Sprinkle into the egg white mixture and blend well.

Drop by small spoonfuls onto a heated, greased Pizelle iron. Close the lid and cook 30 to 45 seconds, until no more steam is escaping and the shell is golden brown. Open the lid and immediately shape the shells around a cannoli tube form or a sanitized broom handle. Be careful because the cannoli will be superhot coming off the iron. I use a fork and then drape the shell around the cannoli form. Let the shells cool on the form before sliding them off. It's helpful to have 4 or 5 cannoli forms so you can continue to bake while the previous batch is cooling.

To make the filling, mix together the ricotta, confectioners' sugar, cream, cinnamon, orange zest, rum, and vanilla until well combined. Stir in the chocolate chips and pistachio nuts.

Right before serving, fill a pastry bag with the filling (or use a zip-top bag with a corner snipped off) and gently squeeze the filling into each end of the shells. If you fill them too early, the shells will soften and may break. Dust with confectioners' sugar and serve.

continued

It isn't necessary to have a Pizelle iron in order to make the shells; it just looks more elegant if you do. If you don't have one, cut a stencil out of a clean plastic tub lid, such as cottage cheese. Trace a 3$^1/_2$-inch circle onto the lid and cut out the inner part you just traced. Lay the stencil on a piece of parchment paper and spread the cookie batter thinly across the stencil. You may only be able to form two or three before the baked shells are too cool to form easily, so it helps to have several pans to rotate in and out of the oven. Bake at 325°F for 2 to 5 minutes, until a nice golden brown.

You can make most of this ahead of time and assemble at the last minute: freeze the baked shells in an airtight container and refrigerate the filling until just before you're planning to serve. If you want to assemble them ahead of time, melt together $^1/_2$ cup of semisweet or dark chocolate and 1$^1/_2$ teaspoons of butter and use a small pastry brush to gently paint the inside of the shells with the mixture. This acts as a barrier to the moisture, and also adds more chocolate flavor!

YAM BISCUITS

{EASY} Makes 12 biscuits

I love the holiday season, beginning with Thanksgiving and ending with New Year's Eve. There's something about the scent of pine needles and burning fireplaces and, of course, spices emanating from every kitchen. This recipe is adapted from a family friend's kitchen. Maria always hosted the biggest Thanksgiving potluck dinners and made these incredible yammy biscuits. There is just a hint of sweetness to them, as well as a touch of holiday spice.

1 whole large yam (about 1 cup / 340 g)

1 cup / 147 g millet flour

1 cup / 170 g sweet white rice flour

1 cup / 130 g tapioca starch

1/2 cup / 113 g firmly packed dark brown sugar

1 tablespoon / 14 g baking powder

3/4 teaspoon / 3.6 g salt

1/2 teaspoon / 1.8 g lemon zest

1/2 teaspoon / 1.3 g cinnamon

1/4 teaspoon / .5 g ground allspice

1/4 teaspoon / .5 g ground nutmeg

1/2 cup / 113 g butter, cold and cubed

3 tablespoons / 42.4 g heavy cream

MAPLE BUTTER

1/2 cup / 133 g butter, room temperature

1/4 cup / 85 g pure maple syrup

2 tablespoons / 18 g confectioners' sugar

Preheat the oven to 425°F. Line a large baking sheet with parchment paper and set aside.

Wash the yam skin and pierce all over with a fork. Bake until a knife easily cuts through the yam, 35 to 40 minutes. Remove from the oven and cool to room temperature. Lower the oven temperature to 325°F.

Combine the flours, tapioca starch, brown sugar, baking powder, salt, lemon zest, cinnamon, allspice, and nutmeg. Using your fingertips (or a food processor), mix in the butter until the mixture resembles coarse pea-sized crumbs. Peel the skin off the yam and mash in a bowl or food processor. Stir the mashed yam into the flour mixture. Add 2 tablespoons of the cream and stir just until moistened.

Shape the dough into a log 2 inches thick. Slice the log every inch into rounds and lay on the baking sheet. Pat gently to flatten. Brush the top of each biscuit with the remaining tablespoon of cream and bake until lightly golden brown, 10 to 12 minutes. A toothpick inserted in the center should come out clean, not doughy. Let cool for 10 minutes.

Meanwhile, make the maple butter. Using a stand mixer with a paddle attachment, beat the butter on medium speed until light, fluffy, and pale in color, up to 5 minutes. Add the maple syrup and confectioners' sugar and blend thoroughly.

While still slightly warm, slather the top of each biscuit with a generous blob of the maple butter and serve.

VANILLA CHIFFON CAKE
WITH BLACKBERRY COULIS

{INTERMEDIATE}   Serves 10

My dad lives at the end of a long dead-end street, one entire side of which is tightly lined with blackberry bushes. The summer I was fourteen, my friend Amy and I spent hours picking the sun-warmed berries and making anything blackberry: blackberry crisp, blackberry milkshakes, and the blackberry sauce that inspired this recipe.

6 egg whites

¹/₄ teaspoon cream of tartar

1¹/₂ cups / 340 g sugar

6 egg yolks

¹/₂ cup / 108 g canola oil

³/₄ cup / 142 g potato starch

²/₃ cup / 85 g tapioca starch

²/₃ cup / 111 g rice flour

1 tablespoon plus 1 teaspoon /
   19 g baking powder

¹/₂ teaspoon / 2.4 g baking soda

¹/₂ teaspoon / 2.4 g salt

¹/₄ teaspoon / .2 g xanthan gum

²/₃ cup / 142 g rice milk

2 teaspoons / 10 g vanilla extract

1¹/₂ cups / 340 g fresh blackberries

VANILLA GLAZE

2 cups / 284 g confectioners' sugar

¹/₄ cup / 57 g rice milk

1 teaspoon / 5 g vanilla extract

Preheat the oven to 300°F. Spray a 10-inch tube pan with gluten-free cooking spray and set aside.

Put the egg whites and cream of tartar in a clean, dry mixing bowl. Using a stand mixer with a whip attachment, beat on medium-high speed until thick and foamy. Slowly sprinkle in 1 cup of the sugar and whip until glossy and medium peaks form. Transfer to another clean, dry bowl. In the first mixing bowl, whip the egg yolks and the remaining ¹/₂ cup of sugar on high speed until pale, light, and tripled in volume and the mixture reaches the "ribbon stage": if you drip a spoonful of the mixture across the surface, it forms a ribbon visible for 3 seconds before it sinks back into the mixture. This takes about 5 minutes. Then blend in the oil until well combined. In a small bowl, combine the starches, rice flour, baking powder, baking soda, salt, and xanthan gum. Fit the mixer with a paddle attachment. Add the dry ingredients to the egg yolk mixture in 3 additions, alternating with the rice milk and vanilla, and blend thoroughly after each addition. Stop the mixer and gently fold in the egg whites, a third at a time.

Pour the batter into the tube pan and bake until a toothpick inserted in the center comes out clean and the top is golden brown, 50 to 60 minutes. Remove from the oven and place on a cooling rack. Let cool about 20 minutes. Run a butter knife around the edge of the pan to loosen the cake and invert the cake onto a serving platter to cool to room temperature, about 30 minutes more.

ingredients and method continued

BLACKBERRY COULIS

2 cups / 453 g fresh or frozen
  blackberries

1/2 cup / 113 g sugar

1/3 cup / 71 ml water

2 teaspoons / 7 g orange zest

1 teaspoon / 5 g lemon juice

To make the glaze, whisk together the confectioners' sugar, rice milk, and vanilla until smooth and shiny. Drizzle over the cooled cake and let set while you make the coulis.

Place all the coulis ingredients in a saucepan and bring to a boil. Simmer over medium-high heat, stirring constantly, until most of the liquid has evaporated, about 5 minutes. Let cool. If you desire a smoother texture, puree in a food processor or strain out the seeds.

Place a tablespoon of the coulis across a dessert plate and put a slice of the cake on top. Top with additional coulis and a few of the fresh berries.

Award-Winning Cupcakes

LITTLE TREATS THAT PACK BIG TASTE

I am often asked about my favorite part of being on *Cupcake Wars*, and my answer is always the same: WINNING! Trite but true. While competing is an exhilarating, exhausting experience, and I learned a lot each time, winning validated gluten-free baking as legitimate—and sometimes even better than traditional baking! I loved being spurred on by the exotic ingredients on the inspiration table and the twisted themes and bringing that inspiration back to the bake shop.

In this chapter, I've included some of the *Cupcake Wars* entries that most impressed judges Candace Nelson and Florian Bellanger, like African Yam Cupcakes, Boston Cream Pie Cupcakes, and Eggnog Cupcakes—as well as a few of my personal favorites, such as the exotically spiced Persian Love Cakes and the celebratory Champagne Cupcakes. No matter which flavor you choose, they're all guaranteed to add a festive flair to your next birthday, book club, soccer game, or any occasion.

AFRICAN YAM CUPCAKES

{INTERMEDIATE}   Makes 24 cupcakes

I was very excited to be invited back to *Cupcake Wars* to participate in their *Cupcake Champions* competition. When the host of the show announced the *Madagascar 3* movie premiere as the theme of our episode, I was delighted. Most of my friends have small children and I had seen the first two *Madagascar* movies myself. My assistant Jackie and I chose to combine the flavors of yams, coffee, and cloves, and the judges loved this slightly sweet yam cake paired with the light airiness of the mascarpone whipped cream.

These cupcakes are delicious without the decorations pictured on the next page, but if you want to try making them, use a vegetable peeler to make peelings from a yam, then heat vegetable oil to 365°F and fry the slices for a few seconds. Using extreme caution, remove and let drain on paper towels for a few seconds, then roll in a mixture of $^1/_4$ cup sugar and $^1/_2$ teaspoon cloves. Make sure to let them cool completely before topping the cupcakes!

$^1/_2$ cup / 113 g butter

$^1/_2$ cup / 113 g granulated sugar

$^1/_2$ cup / 127 g packed brown sugar

2 eggs

$^1/_2$ cup / 67 g tapioca starch

$^1/_2$ cup / 95 g potato starch

$^1/_3$ cup / 55 g rice flour

1 tablespoon / 14 g baking powder

$^1/_4$ teaspoon / 1.2 g salt

$^1/_4$ teaspoon / .2 g xanthan gum

$^1/_2$ teaspoon / 1.3 g cinnamon

$^1/_4$ teaspoon / .5 g ground cloves

$^1/_4$ teaspoon / .4 g ground ginger

$^1/_3$ cup / 76 g milk

$^3/_4$ cup / 255 g mashed roasted yams (canned, or about 1 large fresh yam)

1 tablespoon / 14 g vanilla extract

Preheat the oven to 350°F. Line two 12-cup muffin pans with paper liners and set aside.

Using a stand mixer with a paddle attachment, cream the butter on high speed until very light and fluffy. Add the sugars and beat until very creamy and light. Add the eggs, one at a time, and blend thoroughly, stopping occasionally to scrape down the sides of the bowl. In a separate bowl, combine the starches, rice flour, baking powder, salt, xanthan gum, cinnamon, cloves, and ginger. Add the dry ingredients to the butter mixture in 3 additions, alternating with the milk, and blend thoroughly after each addition, again stopping to scrape down the sides of the bowl. Stir in the yams and vanilla by hand until well blended.

Evenly fill the cupcake liners three-quarters full and bake until a toothpick inserted in the center comes out clean, 14 to 18 minutes. Watch the last 2 minutes to ensure the cakes don't get overbaked and dry. Remove from the oven and place each cupcake on a cooling rack until completely cool, 15 to 30 minutes.

ingredients and method continued

COFFEE PASTRY CREAM

1 cup / 227 g milk

4 tablespoons / 56 g sugar

1 whole egg

1 egg yolk

$^1/_3$ cup / 51 g cornstarch

1 tablespoon / 14 g butter

$^3/_4$ teaspoon / 3.8 g vanilla extract

$1^1/_2$ teaspoons / 17 g concentrated coffee extract

CLOVE MASCARPONE WHIPPED CREAM

8 ounces / 226 g mascarpone cheese

1 cup / 142 g confectioners' sugar

1 teaspoon / 2 g ground cloves

$^2/_3$ cup / 158 g heavy whipping cream

2 tablespoons / 28 g vanilla extract

Pinch / about .5 g salt

To make the pastry cream, line a baking pan with heatproof plastic wrap and set aside. Place the milk and 2 tablespoons of the sugar in a saucepan and scald the milk (heat to the point where it is steaming and the edges look like it is about to boil but is not yet bubbling). Meanwhile, in a large bowl, whisk together the egg, egg yolk, cornstarch, and the remaining 2 tablespoons of sugar until smooth. Once the milk is scalded, whisk the egg mixture vigorously while very slowly pouring in the milk in a steady stream. Then pour the mixture back into the saucepan and return to medium-high heat. Whisk constantly while heating to ensure that no lumps form. Bring to a boil and, whisking constantly, continue to let boil for 90 seconds. Remove from the heat and stir in the butter, vanilla, and coffee extract until well blended.

Pour the pastry cream into the plastic wrap–lined pan and cover the entire surface of the cream with additional plastic wrap to prevent a skin from forming. Chill for 30 to 60 minutes.

To make the whipped cream, using a stand mixer with a whip attachment, mix the mascarpone, confectioners' sugar, and cloves on low speed until well combined. Blend in the cream, vanilla, and salt on low speed, then whip on high speed until thick and moderately stiff.

Fill a pastry bag fitted with a #805 closed star piping tip with the whipped cream and chill until ready to use. If you don't have a pastry bag, you can use a large zip-top bag and snip off a corner to squeeze out the frosting. Remove the plastic wrap from the pastry cream and place the cream in a bowl. Whisk to soften and smooth the texture. Fill a pastry bag with the cream. Using an apple corer or a knife, core out the centers of the cupcakes, about $^1/_2$ inch in diameter, almost to the bottom. Fill the centers with the pastry cream and top with the whipped cream. If desired, each component can be made ahead of time and everything put together at the last minute.

BOSTON CREAM PIE CUPCAKES

{ADVANCED} Makes 24 cupcakes

For years before my friend Sheila went gluten-free, she and her husband, Brad, would celebrate birthdays, Mother's Day, and Father's Day with a Boston cream pie. When Sheila was diagnosed with celiac disease, Brad told her that until she could eat a Boston cream pie, he would also abstain. Soon after I opened my shop, I came up with this recipe so Sheila and Brad could once again enjoy their favorite dessert. Vanilla bean paste (available at specialty natural foods markets) is an infusion of the vanilla bean seeds with vanilla extract. It's thicker than vanilla and adds a deeper, warmer flavor to the pastry cream filling, but feel free to substitute an equal amount of vanilla extract.

1 cup / 226 g butter, room temperature

2 cups / 454 g sugar

4 eggs

1 cup / 130 g tapioca starch

1 cup / 190 g potato starch

2/3 cup / 111 g white rice flour

1 tablespoon plus 1 teaspoon / 19 g baking powder

1/2 teaspoon / 2.4 g salt

1/2 teaspoon / .5 g xanthan gum

1 1/2 cups / 340 g whole milk

2 teaspoons / 10 g vanilla extract

VANILLA BEAN PASTRY CREAM

2 cups / 454 g whole milk

1/2 cup / 226 g sugar

6 egg yolks

1/3 cup / 51 g cornstarch

2 tablespoons / 28 g butter, room temperature

2 teaspoons / 28 g vanilla bean paste

Preheat the oven to 375°F. Line two 12-cup muffin pans with paper liners and set aside.

Using a stand mixer with a paddle attachment, beat the butter on medium speed until light in color and very fluffy. Add the sugar and beat until light and creamy, stopping occasionally to scrape down the sides of the bowl. Add the eggs, one at a time, and blend thoroughly, scraping down the sides of the bowl at the end. In a separate bowl, combine the starches, rice flour, baking powder, salt, and xanthan gum. Add the dry ingredients to the butter mixture in 3 additions, alternating with the milk and vanilla in 2 additions, stopping occasionally to scrape down the sides of the bowl and blending thoroughly after each, but being careful not to overmix.

Evenly fill the cupcake liners two-thirds full and bake until the tops are slightly springy to the touch and a toothpick inserted in the center comes out clean, 13 to 16 minutes. Remove from the oven and place each cupcake on a cooling rack until completely cool.

To make the pastry cream, line a baking pan with heatproof plastic wrap and set aside. Place the milk and 1/4 cup of the sugar in a saucepan and scald the milk (heat to the point where it is steaming and the edges look like it is about to boil

DARK CHOCOLATE BUTTERCREAM

1 cup plus 2 tablespoons / 255 g sugar

¹/₄ cup / 57 g water

4 egg whites

¹/₄ teaspoon cream of tartar

1 cup / 176 g good-quality dark chocolate, chopped

1¹/₂ cups / 340 g butter, room temperature

1 teaspoon / 5 g vanilla bean paste

Pinch / about .5 g fine sea salt

but is not yet bubbling). Meanwhile, in a large bowl, whisk together the egg yolks, cornstarch, and the remaining ¹/₄ cup of sugar until well combined. Once the milk is scalded, whisk the egg mixture vigorously while very slowly pouring in the milk in a steady stream. Then pour the mixture back into the saucepan and return to medium-high heat. Whisk constantly while heating to ensure that no lumps form. Bring to a boil and, whisking constantly, continue to let boil for 90 seconds. Remove from the heat and stir in the butter and vanilla bean paste until well blended.

Pour the pastry cream into the plastic wrap–lined pan and cover the entire surface of the cream with additional plastic wrap to prevent a skin from forming. Chill 30 to 60 minutes.

To make the buttercream, stir together the sugar and water in a heavy saucepan. Wipe down the sides of the pan with a wet pastry brush to ensure that no sugar crystals get in the syrup. Heat until boiling and a candy thermometer reaches 250°F, 15 to 20 minutes. Meanwhile, switching the mixer to a whip attachment, beat the egg whites on medium speed to the soft peak stage (whites will look foamy and white). Be careful not to overwhip. If the whites are beating faster than the sugar mixture is cooking, turn down the mixer speed. Add the cream of tartar and continue whipping. On medium speed, gently pour in the hot sugar syrup. Turn to high and whip until the bowl no longer feels warm to the touch, about 7 minutes. In the meantime, melt the chocolate in a microwave-safe bowl at 30-second intervals, stirring well between each, and set aside. Once the mixing bowl is no longer warm, add the butter in small chunks on medium speed until completely incorporated. Stop the mixer, scrape down the sides of the bowl, and add the vanilla bean paste and salt on medium-low speed until thoroughly

continued

combined. Spoon about $^1/_2$ cup of the buttercream into the chocolate and stir to combine. Add back into the mixing bowl and whip thoroughly on high speed, stopping to scrape down the sides of the bowl to ensure that all the chocolate is combined.

Fit an 18-inch pastry bag with a #847 star tip and twist the bag right by the tip to prevent the buttercream from leaking out. While you grasp the bag right above the star tip with your hand, fold the top of the bag over your hand. Spoon the buttercream into the bag. Remove the plastic wrap from the chilled pastry cream and place the cream in a bowl. Whisk to soften and smooth the texture. Take a pastry bag fitted with a #802 round piping tip and fill it with the cream. Using an apple corer or a knife, core out the centers of the cupcakes, about $^1/_2$ inch in diameter, almost to the bottom. Fill with the pastry cream and frost the tops with the buttercream.

ORANGE-VANILLA DREAMSICLE CUPCAKES

When I first set out to write this book, I intended the cupcake chapter to be full of my acclaimed treats from *Cupcake Wars*. However, my Dreamsicle cupcake kept leaping to mind. Evocative of summertime roller skating and chasing the ice cream truck down the block, I found I couldn't let it go. This particular Dreamsicle won't melt anywhere but in your mouth, and brings to mind joyful summer days whenever you decide to make them.

1 cup / 227 g butter, room temperature

2 cups / 454 g sugar

5 large eggs

1 cup / 130 g tapioca starch

1 cup / 190 g potato starch

3/4 cup / 122 g rice flour

1 tablespoon plus 1 teaspoon / 19 g baking powder

3/4 teaspoon / 3.6 g salt

1/2 teaspoon / .5 g xanthan gum

3/4 cup / 170 ml whole milk

1/2 cup / 150 g orange juice concentrate, thawed

1 tablespoon / 14 g vanilla extract

MASCARPONE FROSTING

1 1/2 cups / 340 g mascarpone cheese

1 cup / 142 g confectioners' sugar

3/4 cup / 178 g heavy cream

1/3 cup / 85 g orange juice concentrate, thawed

1 tablespoon / 14 g vanilla extract

Orange zest, for topping (optional)

Preheat the oven to 325°F. Line two 12-cup muffin pans and one 6-cup muffin pan with paper liners and set aside.

Using a stand mixer with a paddle attachment, cream the butter on high speed until light and fluffy. Cream in the sugar until the mixture is several shades lighter and very fluffy. Add the eggs, one at a time, and blend thoroughly, stopping occasionally to scrape down the sides of the bowl. In a separate bowl, combine the starches, rice flour, baking powder, salt, and xanthan gum. Add the dry ingredients to the butter mixture on low speed in 3 additions, alternating with the milk, mixing as little as possible. Stir in the orange juice and vanilla by hand.

Evenly fill the cupcake liners two-thirds full and bake until a toothpick inserted in the center comes out clean, 14 to 18 minutes. Remove from the oven and place each cupcake on a cooling rack until completely cool.

To make the mascarpone frosting, switch to a whip attachment and slowly blend together the mascarpone and confectioners' sugar until they have a uniform texture. Beat in the cream, half of the orange juice concentrate, and the vanilla on medium-high until the mixture starts to get thick and fluffy, stopping to scrape down the sides of the bowl. Beat in the remaining orange juice until very thick and fluffy, like whipped cream.

Fill a pastry bag fitted with a #805 closed star piping tip with the frosting and chill until ready to use. You can also use a large zip-top bag with the corner snipped off. Frost all the cupcakes, sprinkle with orange zest if you like, and watch the kids roller-skate down the street to get one!

EGGNOG CUPCAKES

{ADVANCED} Makes 12 cupcakes

My earliest memory of drinking eggnog is when I was seven at a holiday party. I carefully helped myself to a crystal glassful from the punch bowl and took it to the window next to the tinseled Christmas tree. There was a sense of anticipation and magic in the air, and whenever I drink eggnog, it takes me back to that party. These days, I make my own eggnog from scratch. You can double the eggnog portion of the recipe if you want to reserve some to drink. The rum is optional but adds a great depth of flavor both to the drink and the cupcakes.

EGGNOG

2 egg yolks

2 tablespoons / 28 g sugar

1/4 cup / 57 g heavy cream

1 1/2 teaspoons / 7.5 g rum

1/8 teaspoon / .6 g vanilla extract

1/8 teaspoon / .3 g ground nutmeg

EGGNOG CAKE

1/2 cup / 67 g tapioca starch

1/2 cup / 95 g potato starch

1/3 cup / 55 g rice flour

2 teaspoons / 10 g baking powder

3/4 teaspoon / 1.7 g ground nutmeg

1/4 teaspoon / .3 g xanthan gum

1/4 teaspoon / 1.2 g salt

1 1/2 cup / 113 g butter, room
    temperature

1/2 cup / 113 g sugar

1 egg

3/4 cup eggnog (see recipe above)

3 tablespoons / 42 g canola oil

1 tablespoon plus 1 teaspoon / 19 g rum

2 teaspoons / 10 g vanilla extract

To make the eggnog, using a stand mixer with a whip attachment, beat the egg yolks and sugar on high speed until very light and fluffy, about 6 minutes. Blend in the cream, rum, vanilla, and nutmeg until frothy and thick.

To make the cake, preheat the oven to 325°F. Line two 12-cup muffin pans with paper liners and set aside.

Combine the starches, rice flour, baking powder, nutmeg, xanthan gum, and salt and set aside. Switching the mixer to a paddle attachment, cream the butter on high speed until light and fluffy. Cream in the sugar until the mixture is several shades lighter and very fluffy. Blend in the egg, scrape down the sides of the bowl, and slowly pour in the eggnog, stopping to scrape down the bowl again. Stir in the oil, rum, and vanilla by hand.

Evenly fill the cupcake liners two-thirds full and bake until a toothpick inserted in the center comes out clean, 14 to 18 minutes. Remove from the oven and place each cupcake on a cooling rack until completely cool.

To make the eggnog pastry cream, line a baking pan with heatproof plastic wrap and set aside. Place the milk and 1/4 cup of the sugar in a saucepan and scald the milk (heat to the point where it is steaming and the edges look like it is about to boil but is not yet bubbling). Meanwhile, in a large bowl, whisk together the egg yolks, cornstarch, and the remaining 1/4 cup of sugar until smooth. Once the milk is scalded, whisk the egg mixture vigorously while very slowly pouring in the milk in a steady stream. Then pour the mixture back into the saucepan and return to medium-high heat.

EGGNOG PASTRY CREAM

2 cups / 454 ml whole milk

1/2 cup / 113 g sugar

4 egg yolks

1/3 cup / 51 g cornstarch

2 tablespoons / 28 g butter

2 teaspoons / 10 g vanilla bean paste
or extract

2 tablespoons / 28 g rum

1/2 teaspoon / 1.1 g ground nutmeg

RUM-NUTMEG BUTTERCREAM

1 cup / 227 g sugar

1/4 cup / 57 g water

4 egg whites

1/2 teaspoon cream of tartar

1 1/2 cups / 340 g butter, room
temperature

3 tablespoons / 43 g rum

1 3/4 teaspoons / 4 g ground nutmeg

1 teaspoon / 5 g vanilla bean paste
or extract

Pinch / .5 g salt

SHORTCUTS

Eggnog: Use store-bought eggnog and decrease the amount of sugar in the cake.

Eggnog Pastry Cream: Mix 2 cups gluten-free vanilla pudding with the rum and nutmeg.

Cake: Replace the starches, flour, baking powder, xanthan gum, and salt with 1 1/3 cups gluten-free all-purpose baking mix.

Whisk constantly while heating to ensure that no lumps form. Bring to a boil and, whisking constantly, continue to let boil for 90 seconds. Remove from the heat and stir in the butter, vanilla bean paste, rum, and nutmeg until well blended.

Pour the pastry cream into the plastic wrap—lined pan and cover the entire surface of the cream with additional plastic wrap to prevent a skin from forming. Chill 30 to 60 minutes.

To make the rum-nutmeg buttercream, stir together the sugar and water in a small saucepan. Wipe down the sides of the pan with a wet pastry brush to ensure that no sugar crystals get in the syrup. Heat until boiling and a candy thermometer registers 248°F. Meanwhile, switching the mixer back to the whip attachment, beat the egg whites and cream of tartar on high speed to the soft peak stage. On medium speed, very slowly pour in the hot sugar syrup. Turn to high and whip until the bowl no longer feels warm to the touch. Add the butter in chunks and mix until fully incorporated, stopping occasionally to scrape down the sides of the bowl. Slowly blend in the rum, nutmeg, vanilla bean paste, and salt.

Fill a pastry bag or large zip-top bag with the buttercream. A pastry piping tip is optional but is a good way to ensure the buttercream comes out evenly. Snip the corner off the bag and set aside.

Remove the plastic wrap from the chilled pastry cream and place the cream in a bowl. Whisk to soften and smooth the texture. Spoon the pastry cream into another pastry bag or large zip-top bag and snip off a corner to squeeze out the cream.

Using an apple corer or a knife, core out the centers of the cupcakes, about 1/2 inch in diameter, almost to the bottom. Fill with the pastry cream. Frost the tops with the buttercream and enjoy!

PERSIAN LOVE CAKES
with CARDAMOM BUTTERCREAM

{INTERMEDIATE}   Makes 20 cupcakes

When I was in my midtwenties, I studied tribal belly dancing. There was always incense burning at the studio, and I would return home each day smelling of a mysterious aroma. I was inspired to create these alluring cupcakes, with the spicy redolence of cardamom, sweet nuttiness of pistachios, and butteriness of saffron. Since gluten-free baking can be pricey enough, I've eliminated the saffron here. If you wish to use it, simply add the saffron threads to the butter in the first step of mixing. You don't need more than $1/4$ teaspoon.

If you want to try making the little heart decorations shown in the photograph, simply tint a bit of the buttercream red and pipe it into a V shape for a cute accent!

$3/4$ cup / 93 g shelled pistachios

$1/3$ cup / 55 g rice flour

$1/3$ cup / 63 g potato starch

$1/3$ cup / 41 g tapioca starch

2 teaspoons / 10 g baking powder

$1^1/2$ teaspoons / 3 g cardamom

$1/4$ teaspoon / .3 g xanthan gum

$1/4$ teaspoon / 1.2 g salt

6 tablespoons / 85 g butter, room temperature

1 cup / 227 g sugar

3 large eggs

$1/2$ cup / 113 g milk

1 tablespoon / 14 g vanilla extract

CARDAMOM BUTTERCREAM

1 cup / 227 g sugar

$1/4$ cup / 57 g water

4 egg whites

$1/4$ teaspoon cream of tartar

$3/4$ cup / 170 g butter

1 teaspoon / 5 g vanilla extract

$3/4$ teaspoon / 1.5 g cardamom

Preheat the oven to 350°F. Line two 12-cup muffin pans with paper liners (enough for 20 cupcakes) and set aside.

Measure the pistachios, rice flour, starches, baking powder, cardamom, xanthan gum, and salt into the bowl of a food processor and pulse until the pistachios are finely ground. Using a stand mixer with a paddle attachment, cream the butter on high speed until light and fluffy. Cream in the sugar until the mixture is several shades lighter and very fluffy. Add the eggs, one at a time, and blend thoroughly, stopping after each addition to scrape down the sides of the bowl. Add the vanilla to the milk. Add the dry ingredients to the butter mixture in 3 additions, alternating with the milk mixture, and blend thoroughly after each addition, stopping occasionally to scrape down the sides of the bowl.

Evenly fill the cupcake liners two-thirds full and bake until a toothpick inserted in the center comes out clean, 14 to 18 minutes. Remove from the oven and place each cupcake on a cooling rack until completely cool.

To make the cardamom buttercream, stir together the sugar and water in a small saucepan. Wipe down the sides of the pan with a wet pastry brush to ensure that no sugar crystals get in the syrup. Heat until boiling and a candy thermometer registers 248°F, about 10 minutes.

continued

Meanwhile, switching the mixer to a whip attachment, beat the egg whites and cream of tartar on high speed to the soft peak stage. On medium speed, very slowly pour in the hot sugar syrup. Turn to high and whip until the bowl no longer feels warm to the touch. Add the butter in chunks and mix until fully incorporated, stopping occasionally to scrape down the sides of the bowl. Slowly blend in the vanilla and cardamom.

Frost the cooled cupcakes with the buttercream and enjoy!

CHAMPAGNE CUPCAKES

{ADVANCED}   Makes 24 cupcakes

I've been making champagne cake for as long as I've been baking, and I've been making these cupcakes for as long as I've been gluten-free. When I was twelve years old, I made my mom's surprise fortieth birthday cake. The flavor? Yep. You guessed it! Champagne. Now that I'm an adult myself, these cupcakes make me want to put on a little black dress and heels, drape myself with sparkling jewelry, and dance the night away—but there's no need to wait until New Year's Eve to enjoy these! The carbonation in the champagne makes the cake so light and airy. The flavor is delicately boozy and sweet, but if you prefer, you can swap in sparkling cider for the champagne: just reduce the amount of sugar in the cake to $1^1/_2$ cups.

1 cup / 227 g butter, room
    temperature

2 cups / 454 g sugar

4 large eggs

1 cup / 130 g tapioca starch

1 cup / 190 g potato starch

$^2/_3$ cup / 111 g rice flour

1 tablespoon plus 1 teaspoon /
    19 g baking powder

$^1/_2$ teaspoon / .5 g xanthan gum

$^1/_2$ teaspoon / 2.4 g sea salt

$1^1/_2$ cups / 340 ml brut champagne
    or prosecco or sparkling wine

CHAMPAGNE FRENCH BUTTERCREAM

2 cups / 454 g sugar

$^1/_4$ cup / 57 g water

10 egg yolks

$2^1/_2$ cups / 567 g butter, room
    temperature

$^1/_3$ cup / 76 g champagne

Preheat the oven to 350°F. Line two 12-cup muffin pans with paper liners and set aside.

Using a stand mixer with a paddle attachment, cream the butter on high speed until light and fluffy. Cream in the sugar until the mixture is several shades lighter and very fluffy. Add the eggs, one at a time, and blend thoroughly, stopping after each addition to scrape down the sides of the bowl. In a separate bowl, combine the starches, rice flour, baking powder, xanthan gum, and salt. Add the dry ingredients to the butter mixture in 3 additions, alternating with the champagne, and blend thoroughly after each addition, stopping occasionally to scrape down the sides of the bowl.

Evenly fill the cupcake liners two-thirds full and bake until a toothpick inserted in the center comes out clean, 14 to 18 minutes. Remove from the oven and place each cupcake on a cooling rack until completely cool.

To make the champagne buttercream, stir together the sugar and water in a small saucepan. Wipe down the sides

continued

of the pan with a wet pastry brush to ensure that no sugar crystals get in the syrup. Heat until boiling and a candy thermometer registers 248°F. Meanwhile, switching the mixer to a whip attachment, beat the egg yolks on high speed until light, fluffy, and tripled in volume. On medium speed, very slowly pour in the hot sugar syrup. Turn to high and whip until the bowl no longer feels warm to the touch, about 10 minutes. Add the butter in chunks and mix until fully incorporated, stopping occasionally to scrape down the sides of the bowl. Slowly blend in the champagne.

Frost the cooled cupcakes with the buttercream. I like to sprinkle a bit of edible disco dust over the top for a glittery, festive touch!

Tarts, Pies, and Puffs

DESSERTS TO IMPRESS

My husband, Jason, and I love to entertain. When the weather is nice, we set out a table-cloth on our patio table, turn on the string lights, and invite friends over. Jason is in charge of the main course, as he loves to grill, and I take care of the dessert. Since it's the very last experience of a dinner party, it's always fun to make something memorable.

I love preparing fancier desserts that can take a few days to make. I assemble every-thing ahead of time so all I have to do when our guests arrive is pour the wine and clear the plates before bringing out dessert. With the recipes in this chapter, rest assured that your guests will be impressed with what you've made—whether or not you disclose that it happens to be gluten-free!

MEXICAN CHOCOLATE BAKED ALASKA

{ADVANCED}   Makes 20 servings

I have always been spellbound by a really good baked Alaska, and it's one of those desserts that looks very dramatic to guests. Traditional baked Alaska usually comes with strawberry ice cream, but I am a huge fan of Mexican chocolate "spice cream," which we make from scratch at the bake shop for our summertime-favorite ice cream sandwiches. If you don't have the time or desire to make your ice cream from scratch, see the sidebar on page 101 for a shortcut. There are a few steps to this recipe and it can take some time to put together, but you can assemble the dessert ahead of time and store in an airtight container in the freezer. Simply torch the meringue or stick under the broiler for 30 to 45 seconds just before serving.

CHOCOLATE SPICED ICE CREAM

3 cups / 714 ml heavy whipping cream

2¹/₂ tablespoons / 19.5 g cinnamon

¹/₂ teaspoon / .9 g cayenne pepper

Pinch / .5 g salt

1¹/₂ teaspoons / 7.5 g vanilla extract

1¹/₂ cups / 340 g sugar

¹/₄ cup / 21 g natural cocoa powder

12 egg yolks

1²/₃ cups / 378 ml whole milk

CINNAMON ALMOND CAKE BASE

3 eggs

1 cup / 110 g almond flour or powdered almonds

¹/₂ cup / 71 g confectioners' sugar

¹/₄ cup / 21 g natural cocoa powder

2 tablespoons / 21 g potato starch

1 tablespoon / 8 g tapioca starch

1 teaspoon / 2.6 g cinnamon

MERINGUE

9 egg whites

³/₄ teaspoon cream of tartar

¹/₂ cup plus 1 tablespoon / 127 g sugar

To make the ice cream, in a large bowl, stir together the cream, cinnamon, cayenne, salt, and vanilla and set aside. In a heatproof metal bowl, combine the sugar and cocoa powder. Add the egg yolks and whisk until smooth. Set aside. Heat the milk in a saucepan over medium heat until the milk is steaming and small bubbles form against the edges of the pan. Whisking the egg mixture constantly, *very* slowly pour in the steaming milk in a steady stream. Don't rush this step. Then pour the milk-egg mixture back into the saucepan and, whisking constantly, heat over medium heat until it just starts to thicken. The mixture is ready when a candy thermometer reaches 180°F or when, upon tilting the pan, you can see that the mixture slightly coats the bottom. Remove from the heat and pour through a strainer into the heavy cream mixture. Stir well. Refrigerate overnight to let the flavors develop.

The next day, freeze a 10-inch-diameter metal mixing bowl or, if you prefer individual-sized baked Alaskas, two muffin pans so that the finished ice cream can go right into a cold container to prevent melting. Remove the ice cream base from the refrigerator and stir. Then freeze according to the directions for your ice cream maker. Spray the frozen mixing bowl or muffin pans with gluten-free cooking spray and line the bowl or 20 of the muffin cups with heavy-duty

continued

SHORTCUT VERSION OF SPICED ICE CREAM

2 pints top-quality chocolate ice cream

2 tablespoons / 15.6 g cinnamon

1/4 teaspoon / .4 g cayenne pepper

Leave the ice cream on the kitchen counter until slightly softened, about 20 minutes. Using a stand mixer with a paddle attachment, scrape the ice cream out of the containers into the mixing bowl and beat in the cinnamon and cayenne just until combined.

plastic wrap. Spoon the ice cream evenly into the bowl or the cups and freeze until solid, about 2 hours.

To make the cake base, preheat the oven to 325°F. Line a 14 by 16-inch jelly roll pan or baking sheet with parchment paper and set aside.

Using a stand mixer with a whip attachment, beat the eggs on high speed until pale yellow, thick, fluffy, and tripled in volume, 5 to 8 minutes. Sprinkle the almond flour over the eggs and blend on low speed. Mix in the confectioners' sugar, cocoa powder, starches, and cinnamon until combined.

Carefully spread the batter evenly over the bottom of the pan in a thin layer, about 1/4 inch thick. Bake just until set, 8 to 10 minutes. Let cool about 5 minutes. Cut out a 10-inch circle for a large baked Alaska, or use a 3-inch biscuit cutter to make 20 small circles for individual servings. It's okay if the base breaks apart— it's just to hold the ice cream. Arrange the circle(s) on a clean baking pan or serving platter and freeze until ready to assemble. If you freeze the platter or plates you plan to use for serving, the dessert will hold up better. Don't do this, though, if you will be browning the meringue under the broiler.

To make the meringue, in a clean, dry mixing bowl, beat the egg whites and cream of tartar to the medium peak stage. Slowly add the sugar and beat until glossy and light and medium-firm peaks hold. Spoon into a pastry bag fitted with a round tip or a gallon-sized ziplock bag with a corner snipped off. Twist the top of the bag or seal to close it.

To assemble, remove the cake base from the freezer and turn onto the serving platter or plates (which must be ovenproof if using the broiler). Remove the parchment paper if not already discarded. Center the ice cream on top of the base. Dot with swirls or pearls of the meringue and cover the entire outside. Use a kitchen torch or put under the broiler for a minute or two until the meringue puffs up and turns golden brown. Serve immediately, or freeze in an airtight container for up to 2 weeks.

COCONUT CREAM PIE

{INTERMEDIATE}   Makes one 9-inch pie or 48 mini pielettes

My dad loves coconut cream pie, so naturally I had to develop a recipe for him. Using thicker shavings of toasted coconut on top imparts a deeper, more memorable flavor and an elegant appearance. You can make one large pie or do as we do at the bake shop and make mini pielettes. I've used coconut in three different forms to impart a very distinctive (and natural) flavor throughout. As a bonus, it's completely dairy-free! Make sure you're using coconut *butter* and not coconut *oil*, which will result in a greasy piecrust. I especially like Artisana coconut butter.

PIECRUST

¹/₂ cup / 74 g millet flour

1¹/₂ teaspoons / 5 g sweet white rice flour

¹/₂ cup / 95 g potato starch

¹/₄ cup / 31 g tapioca starch

2 tablespoons / 28 g sugar

1 teaspoon / 1 g xanthan gum

¹/₂ teaspoon / 2.4 g sea salt

1 cup / 210 g coconut butter, very cold

¹/₄ to ¹/₃ cup / 57 to 76 g very cold water

To make the piecrust, preheat the oven to 375°F. In a large bowl, combine the flours, starches, sugar, xanthan gum, and salt. Using your fingertips (or a food processor), quickly blend in the coconut butter until the mixture resembles coarse pea-sized crumbs. Add just enough of the water to make a handful of dough stick together when you squeeze it.

To make as a whole pie, press the crust into the bottom and sides of a 9-inch pie pan. Bake until crisp and golden brown, 25 to 30 minutes. To make as mini pielettes, line two 24-cup mini muffin pans with mini liners. Place a table-spoon of piecrust into each liner and press into the bottom. Bake until crisp and lightly golden brown, 10 to 15 minutes. Let piecrust cool completely.

To make the pastry cream, spread the shaved coconut evenly on a baking sheet and bake at 350°F for 15 to 20 minutes, stirring every 7 minutes or so, until golden brown. Set aside. Pour the 2 tablespoons of cold water in a small dish. Sprinkle the gelatin over the top and let sit several minutes until the gelatin "blooms" and turns from opaque powder to almost clear. Pour the coconut milk and ¹/₄ cup of the sugar into a saucepan, stir, and scald over medium heat (to the point where it is steaming and small bubbles form at the edge of the pan but it is not actually boiling). Mean-while, in a bowl, whisk together the remaining ¹/₄ cup of sugar, the egg yolks, and the cornstarch until smooth. Once

COCONUT PASTRY CREAM

1/3 cup / 34 g shaved coconut

2 tablespoons / 28 g cold water

1 teaspoon / 1.2 g powdered gelatin

1 (14-ounce / 397 ml) can
coconut milk

1/2 cup / 113 g sugar

4 egg yolks

Scant 1/4 cup / 35 g cornstarch

3/4 cup / 68 g shredded coconut

2 tablespoons / 26 g coconut
butter, room temperature

1 1/2 teaspoons / 7.5 g vanilla bean
paste or extract

4 egg whites

the milk is scalded, whisk the egg mixture vigorously while slowly pouring in the milk in a steady stream. Then pour the mixture back into the saucepan and return to medium heat. Whisk constantly while heating to ensure that no lumps form. Bring to a boil and, whisking constantly, continue to let boil for 60 seconds. Remove from the heat and stir in the hydrated gelatin. Stir in the shredded coconut, coconut butter, and vanilla bean paste until well blended. Set the pan into a large bowl of ice water to immediately chill the mixture, or let sit until cool to the touch. In a clean, dry bowl, whip the egg whites to medium-stiff peaks and gently fold into the coconut pastry cream, one-third at a time.

Gently fill the pie shell with the coconut cream. Or if you're making the pielettes, put the cream in a pastry bag, snip a half inch off the tip, and carefully fill the mini liners. Top with a sprinkle of the toasted coconut and chill until ready to serve.

HAZELNUT PEAR TART
with GOAT CHEESE WHIPPED CREAM

{INTERMEDIATE}   Makes 12 servings

My home state of Oregon is renowned for its filberts (also called hazelnuts), as well as for its fabulous pears grown in the many orchards dotting the countryside. You'll find them both in this tart, which uses the hazelnuts in a variation on the almond cream, or *crème d'amande*, called for in many French pastries. You can use any variety of pear you like; my preference is red d'Anjou. Because there are so many steps to this recipe, I find myself making it over the course of several days. I make the crust the first day and freeze it. The second day, I make the port wine glaze and the hazelnut cream and keep the cream-filled tart in the refrigerator. The day I'm planning to serve, I sauté the pears and make the goat cheese whipped cream (the only element that can't be prepared ahead of time). Breaking it into smaller steps makes the process less daunting. If you don't tolerate eggs well, you can easily omit them from the hazelnut cream: just skip the baking step and keep the tart well chilled. The filling will be less fluffy and more dense and creamy, but still delicious.

HAZELNUT SHORTCRUST

³/₄ cup / 122 g sweet white rice flour

¹/₂ cup / 74 g millet flour

¹/₂ cup / 67 g tapioca starch

¹/₃ cup / 44 g ground hazelnuts or hazelnut meal

¹/₂ teaspoon / .5 g xanthan gum

¹/₄ teaspoon / 1.2 g salt

1 cup / 227 g butter, room temperature

¹/₂ cup / 71 g confectioners' sugar

1 teaspoon / 5 g vanilla extract

To make the shortcrust, using a stand mixer with a paddle attachment, mix together the flours, tapioca starch, ground hazelnuts, xanthan gum, and salt. Mix in the butter, confectioners' sugar, and vanilla on low speed just long enough to make a soft dough. Do not overmix! If the dough is crumbly, that's okay: it will soften as you press it into the tart pan. Divide the dough in half and wrap one half in plastic wrap. Store in an airtight bag in the freezer for up to 3 months (or make the Chocolate Hazelnut Tart on page 108). Press the remaining dough into a 9-inch tart pan with a removable bottom so the dough covers the bottom and sides of the pan. Make sure the dough is only about ¹/₄ inch thick, especially in the corners. Pierce the bottom of the shortcrust all over with a fork and freeze until firm, at least an hour.

Preheat the oven to 425°F. Crumple up a 14 by 16-inch sheet of parchment paper and smooth out again. Place the paper on top of the dough and fill with pie weights or dried beans (if you use beans, don't plan to eat them afterward, as they will be inedible). Bake until golden brown and dry to

HAZELNUT CREAM

1 cup / 133 g ground hazelnuts or hazelnut meal

$^1/_2$ cup / 113 g sugar

$^1/_4$ cup / 31 g tapioca starch

2 eggs

$^1/_2$ cup / 113 g butter, softened

2 teaspoons / 10 g vanilla extract

PEAR FILLING

8 large pears

$^2/_3$ cup / 151 g sugar

1$^1/_2$ teaspoons / 3 g ground cardamom

$^1/_4$ teaspoon / .5 g ground cloves

Pinch / .5 g salt

$^1/_4$ cup / 57 g butter

PORT WINE GLAZE

1 bottle (750 ml) good-quality port wine

1$^1/_2$ cups / 340 g sugar

GOAT CHEESE WHIPPED CREAM

4 ounces / 113 g soft goat cheese

$^1/_2$ cup / 71 g confectioners' sugar

1 cup / 238 g heavy whipping cream

1 teaspoon / 5 g vanilla extract

the touch, 15 to 20 minutes. Lift off the weights and parchment paper and let the crust cool for about 15 minutes.

To make the hazelnut cream, using the mixer and a clean mixing bowl, mix together the ground hazelnuts, sugar, and tapioca starch. Add the eggs, butter, and vanilla and blend on low speed until smooth. Spread the cream evenly over the cooled shortcrust (or chill if you are making the components ahead of time). Pop into a 325°F oven for 16 to 25 minutes. When the filling is baked, it should look golden brown, airy, and firm, almost like a pancake. Let cool for an hour before placing in the refrigerator to set the filling for an additional hour (or up to overnight).

To make the pear filling, core the pears and cut into $^1/_4$-inch slices. Put the pears in a large bowl. In a small bowl, combine the sugar, cardamom, cloves, and salt. Sprinkle over the pears and gently toss or stir to evenly disperse the sugar and spices. In 2 to 3 batches (to avoid overcrowding your pan), sauté the pears in the butter over medium heat, stirring occasionally, until caramelized and soft with a hint of golden brown on the sides, about 15 to 25 minutes per batch.

Remove from the sauté pan and spread over a baking pan to cool.

To make the port glaze, in a small saucepan, combine the wine and sugar over medium-high heat. Bring to a boil to melt the sugar, then turn the heat to medium and keep at a simmer (tiny bubbles should appear at the edges of the pan but the liquid should not reach a rolling boil). Stirring occasionally, reduce the liquid until it is thick and fills a 1-cup measure, about 40 minutes. Remove from the heat and let cool.

continued

To make the whipped cream, crumble the goat cheese into a mixing bowl. Using the mixer with a whip attachment, beat in the confectioners' sugar on low speed just until blended. Add the cream and vanilla and turn to high. Beat until very thick and creamy and medium peaks form.

When you're ready to serve, top the chilled hazelnut cream with the caramelized pears, evenly spread over the tart. Serve each slice topped with a scoop of whipped cream and a drizzle of the port glaze.

CHOCOLATE HAZELNUT TART

{INTERMEDIATE}   Makes 1 Kyra-sized tart (or, if I decide to share, 12 servings)

The idea for this dessert arose while I was creating the Hazelnut Pear Tart on page 104. I had a little extra shortcrust and I thought, "What better way to use it up than to combine it with milk chocolate!" I adore the combination of chocolate and hazelnut, and I used to eat that famous spread with a spoon, straight out of the jar. In fact, when my husband and I got married, one of my vows was a promise to love him more than I love Nutella! Use the best-quality chocolate you can find; it really does make a difference. And a bit of advice: while none of the elements in this recipe is particularly difficult to make, assembling the whole thing is time consuming and sometimes takes me days to prepare. Plan accordingly.

MILK CHOCOLATE GANACHE

1¹/₂ cups / 263 g milk chocolate

1 cup / 238 g heavy cream

HAZELNUT SHORTCRUST

³/₄ cup / 122 g sweet white rice flour

¹/₂ cup / 74 g millet flour

¹/₂ cup / 67 g tapioca starch

¹/₃ cup / 44 g ground hazelnuts or hazelnut meal

¹/₂ teaspoon / .5 g xanthan gum

¹/₄ teaspoon / 1.2 g salt

1 cup / 227 g butter, room temperature

¹/₂ cup / 71 g confectioners' sugar

1 teaspoon / 5 g vanilla extract

To make the ganache, place the milk chocolate in a bowl. Put the heavy cream in a small saucepan over medium heat until scalded (to the point where it is steaming and the edges look like it is about to boil but is not yet bubbling). Do not boil. Pour the scalded cream over the milk chocolate. Let it sit a moment and then stir to combine. Set aside to cool to the consistency of softened peanut butter, about 4 hours at room temperature or 30 to 60 minutes in the fridge. Stir occasionally.

To make the shortcrust, using a stand mixer with a paddle attachment, mix together the flours, tapioca starch, ground hazelnuts, xanthan gum, and salt. Mix in the butter, confectioners' sugar, and vanilla on low speed just long enough to make a soft dough. Do not overmix. If the dough is crumbly, that's okay: it will soften as you press it into the tart pan. Divide the dough in half and wrap one half in plastic wrap. Store in an airtight bag in the freezer for up to three months (or make the Hazelnut Pear Tart on page 104). Press the remaining dough into a 9-inch tart pan with a removable bottom so the dough covers the bottom and sides of the pan. Make sure the dough is only about ¹/₄ inch thick, especially in the corners. Pierce the bottom of the shortcrust all over with a fork and freeze until firm, at least an hour.

HAZELNUT CREAM

1 cup / 133 g ground hazelnuts or hazelnut meal

$^{1}/_{2}$ cup / 113 g sugar

$^{1}/_{4}$ cup / 31 g tapioca starch

2 eggs

$^{1}/_{2}$ cup / 113 g butter, softened

2 teaspoons / 10 g vanilla extract

CANDIED HAZELNUTS

$^{1}/_{2}$ cup / 43 g chopped hazelnuts

3 tablespoons / 42 g sugar

$^{1}/_{4}$ teaspoon / .7 g cinnamon

Preheat the oven to 425°F. Crumple up a 14 by 16-inch sheet of parchment paper and smooth out again. Place the paper on top of the dough and fill with pie weights or dried beans (if you use beans, don't plan to eat them afterward, as they will be inedible). Bake until golden brown and dry to the touch, 15 to 20 minutes. Lift off the weights and parchment paper and let the crust cool for about 15 minutes.

To make the hazelnut cream, using the mixer and a clean mixing bowl, mix together the ground hazelnuts, sugar, and tapioca starch. Pour the hazelnut mixture into a mixing bowl. Add the eggs, butter, and vanilla and blend on low speed until smooth. Spread the cream evenly over the cooled shortcrust (or chill if you are making the components ahead of time). Pop into a 325°F degree oven for 16 to 25 minutes. When the filling is baked, it should look golden brown, airy, and firm, almost like a pancake.

Let cool for about 30 minutes and then place in the refrigerator to set the filling, about an hour (or up to overnight).

To make the candied hazelnuts, place all of the ingredients in a small saucepan over medium heat, stirring constantly. The sugar will caramelize and melt into the hazelnuts, and they will turn dark golden brown and toasty. This will take 5 to 8 minutes, depending on how hot your stovetop runs. Remove the nuts from the saucepan and spread out evenly on a baking sheet until cool to the touch, about 30 minutes. Then roll the nuts around to break up any clusters.

Once the hazelnut cream has set, pour or spread the ganache over the filling and chill to set, 1 to 2 hours (or up to overnight). Sprinkle the hazelnuts liberally over the ganache and chill until you are ready to serve.

CLASSIC CREAM PUFFS

{INTERMEDIATE}   Makes 36 cream puffs

I got the idea for gluten-free cream puffs from my friend and mentor Laura Russell, who writes the gluten-free column for the *Oregonian*. She came up with a tapioca-based recipe for Brazilian cheese puffs, and the dough base reminded me of the pâté à choux used for traditional cream puffs, except that it's much easier to make. The pastry cream can be made up to 5 days in advance; simply keep in an airtight container or wrap well with plastic wrap directly on the cream to keep a skin from forming. The puffs can be baked up to a week ahead and frozen in an airtight container. Make sure you poke the hole in the bottom, sticking your pinky in to clear the way for the filling, before you freeze them. Then, just reheat the puffs at 350°F for 6 to 10 minutes. The assembled puffs can also be frozen in an airtight container, but they will soften quite a bit. Thaw them at room temperature for about 2 hours before you plan to serve them.

PASTRY CREAM

2 cups / 454 ml whole milk

1/2 cup / 113 g sugar

4 egg yolks

1/3 cup / 51 g cornstarch

2 tablespoons / 28 g butter

2 teaspoons / 10 g vanilla bean paste
   or extract

PUFF DOUGH

2 cups / 454 ml whole milk

2/3 cup / 147 g canola oil

4 cups / 521 g tapioca starch

6 eggs

1 tablespoon / 14 g vanilla extract

Pinch / .5 g salt

CHOCOLATE GLAZE

1 1/2 cups / 263 g best-quality dark
   chocolate

1/4 cup / 57 g butter

1/4 cup / 59 g heavy cream

To make the pastry cream, line a baking pan with heatproof plastic wrap and set aside. Place the milk and 1/4 cup of the sugar in a saucepan and scald the milk (heat to the point where it is steaming and the edges look like it is about to boil but is not yet bubbling). Meanwhile, in a large bowl, whisk together the egg yolks, cornstarch, and the remaining 1/4 cup of sugar until smooth. Once the milk is scalded, whisk the egg mixture vigorously while very slowly pouring in the milk in a steady stream. Then pour the mixture back into the saucepan and return to medium-high heat. Whisk constantly while heating to ensure that no lumps form. Bring to a boil and, whisking constantly, continue to let boil for 90 seconds. Remove from the heat and stir in the butter and vanilla bean paste until well blended.

Pour the pastry cream into the plastic wrap–lined pan and cover the entire surface of the cream with additional plastic wrap to prevent a skin from forming. Chill 30 to 60 minutes.

To make the puff dough, preheat the oven to 350°F. Set aside two mini muffin pans and leave them ungreased.

continued

SHORTCUT

To cut down on preparation time, you can use a gluten-free vanilla pudding mix, cooked according to directions. Please do not use an instant mix: the scalded milk is an important flavor enhancer and tastes so much better!

Pour the milk and oil into a small saucepan and bring to a boil. Meanwhile, put the tapioca starch in the mixing bowl of a stand mixer with a paddle attachment. When the milk mixture comes to a boil, turn the mixer on medium speed and slowly pour the milk into the tapioca. Turn to high and add the eggs, one at a time, and blend thoroughly, stopping occasionally to scrape down the sides of the bowl. Mix in the vanilla and salt.

Evenly fill 36 muffin cups two-thirds full. Bake until puffed and golden brown and hard to the touch, about 25 minutes. Meanwhile, remove the plastic wrap from the pastry cream and place the cream in a bowl. Whisk to soften and smooth the texture. Spoon the cream into a pastry bag fitted with a #802 round piping tip. (Normally, I advocate using a ziplock bag if you don't have a pastry bag, but in this instance, the ziplock is likely to split along the seam.) Then refrigerate. Once cool to the touch, pop the puffs out of the pan. (If you can't get the puffs to easily pop out, or if they begin deflating as they cool, put them back in the oven for 5 to 10 minutes so they finish baking and crisp up.) Take a pointed paring knife and carefully cut a small round hole in the bottom of each puff. To fill the cream puffs, insert the piping tip of the bag of pastry cream partway into the bottom of each puff and gently squeeze.

To make the chocolate glaze, melt the chocolate over a double boiler or in a microwave-safe bowl. If using the microwave, heat in 30-second intervals, stirring between each. Stir the butter and cream into the melted chocolate until well blended.

Dip the top of each cream puff in the chocolate glaze, turn right side up, and place directly on a serving platter.

MASCARPONE CHEESECAKE WITH **STRAWBERRY COULIS**

{EASY}   Makes 12 servings

Cheesecake was one of those desserts that always intimidated me. How do you know when it is finished baking, *before* it cracks? The first time I ever dared to make cheesecake for a crowd was for a friend's thirtieth birthday. I had just enrolled in pastry school, and I decided to make a light, cream mascarpone cheesecake. It cracked across the top (my oven was too hot), so I improvised with a strawberry sauce to hide the cracks. No one ever knew I'd had a problem with the recipe: they just thought it was delicious. And no one knew it was gluten-free until I cut a big wedge for myself. Much later, a variation of this cheesecake recipe helped me win *Cupcake Wars*—I guess practice makes better!

GINGER COOKIE CRUST

3 cups / 241 g gluten-free ginger
 cookie crumbs (about 8 Ginger
 Molasses Cookies from page 46)

1/2 cup / 113 g butter, melted

CREAM CHEESE FILLING

2 (8-ounce) bricks / 454 g cream
 cheese, room temperature

1²/3 cups / 391 g mascarpone cheese

4 eggs

1¹/4 cups / 283 g sugar

1 tablespoon / 14 g lemon juice

1/4 teaspoon / 1.2 g salt

Preheat the oven to 325°F. Spray a 9-inch springform pan with gluten-free cooking spray and set aside.

To make the crust, place the cookie crumbs in a food processor and pulse until finely ground. Pour into a bowl and stir in the butter. Press the mixture evenly inside the bottom of the springform pan and bake until golden and crisp, about 20 minutes.

Meanwhile, make the filling. Using a stand mixer with a paddle attachment, beat the cream cheese on medium-high speed until light and fluffy, stopping occasionally to scrape down the sides of the bowl. Continue beating for up to 15 minutes, until no lumps remain. The smoother the cream cheese gets before you add any other ingredients, the silkier your finished cheesecake will be! Beat in the mascarpone until fully blended with the cream cheese, again stopping to scrape down the sides of the bowl. Add the eggs, one at a time, blending thoroughly after each addition. Mix in the sugar, lemon juice, and salt until creamy and smooth.

Place the springform pan with the hot baked crust on a baking sheet (in case the filling leaks). Pour the cream cheese mixture over the crust and bake until just set and all jiggles as one, 60 to 75 minutes or when the tip of a stainless steel knife carefully inserted in the center comes out clean. (If you notice that the cheesecake is cracking,

STRAWBERRY COULIS

1 cup / 167 g frozen strawberries or strawberry puree, thawed

1/2 cup / 113 g sugar

1/3 cup / 76 g water

1 teaspoon / 14 g lemon juice

you can lower the oven temperature by 25 degrees, but this may lengthen the cooking time.) Let cool to room temperature. Then wrap the pan in plastic wrap or cover with aluminum foil and chill until cold, at least two hours or overnight.

To make the coulis, place all of the ingredients in a saucepan and bring just to a boil. Simmer over medium-high heat, stirring constantly, until most of the liquid has evaporated, about 5 minutes. Let cool. If you desire a smoother texture, puree in a food processor or strain out the seeds.

Pour into a shallow bowl and cool completely.

It is easiest to unmold the cheesecake and get it to release from the pan when it is well chilled. Dip a small offset spatula or butter knife in hot water and gently run the knife around the inner edge of the pan. Unlatch the spring and gently remove the outer ring. Place the cheesecake on a serving plate and pour the strawberry coulis over the top. Gently spread the coulis over the cheesecake if you like. Chill until you are ready to serve. I have always found it easiest to cut a very cold (or frozen!) cheesecake using unflavored dental floss. Take a long piece of floss and wrap one end around your index finger on each hand. Pull taut and in one smooth motion, cut the cheesecake in half. Turn the pan 180 degrees and cut in half again. Then cut each wedge into 3 equal portions to make 12 slices.

LILIKOI CHIFFON PIE

{ADVANCED}   Makes 12 servings

My husband and I went to Kauai to celebrate our fifth anniversary. One balmy night after a stroll along the ocean, we had dinner at the Hukilau Lanai, known on the island as a special-occasion restaurant for tourists and locals alike. After a lovely, relaxing (gluten-free!) meal, we indulged in the housemade lilikoi chiffon pie. Lilikoi, the Hawaiian name for passion fruit, is a tart fruit also known as maracaya or maracuja. Look for a puree that is 90 percent passion fruit and 10 percent sugar. You can easily make this recipe dairy-free—simply use coconut butter instead of dairy butter.

MACADAMIA COCONUT CRUST

1 1/2 cups / 288 g macadamia nut pieces

1/2 cup / 46 g sweetened flaked coconut

1/2 cup / 113 g sugar

2 egg whites

LILIKOI FILLING

1/4 cup / 57 g cold water

1 tablespoon / 3.5 g powdered gelatin

6 egg yolks

3/4 cup / 170 g sugar

1/3 cup / 74 g passion fruit puree

1/3 cup / 75 g cold butter, cut into pieces

5 egg whites

RASPBERRY COULIS

About 1 1/2 cups / 227 g fresh or frozen raspberries

1/4 cup / 57 g sugar

3 tablespoons / 47 g water

1 1/2 teaspoons / 7 g passion fruit juice

Preheat the oven to 350°F.

To make the crust, put the macadamia nut pieces and the coconut on a baking sheet and bake until lightly golden brown, about 6 minutes. Remove from the oven and transfer the nuts and coconut to the bowl of a food processor. Add the sugar and pulse until the nuts are a fine meal and the mixture has the texture of coarse sand. Add the egg whites and pulse to combine.

Press the nut mixture into the bottom and up the sides of a 10-inch springform pan. Freeze until firm, about 1 hour. Preheat the oven to 350°F and bake the crust until golden brown, 15 to 20 minutes. Let cool completely.

Meanwhile, make the filling. Place the water in a small dish and sprinkle the gelatin over the surface. Give the dish a little swirl to ensure that all of the gelatin is moistened, and set aside. In a metal bowl over a double boiler on medium-high heat, warm the egg yolks and 1/2 cup of the sugar, whisking constantly until the sugar crystals dissolve. Slowly drizzle in the passion fruit puree and continue whisking until the mixture thickens, 5 to 8 minutes. It should change from looking like juice to looking like lemon curd. Add the butter a piece at a time, whisking until it dissolves and continuing to whisk until all the butter is combined and the mixture is thick and silky. Remove the bowl from the double boiler. Stir in the gelatin until well blended and set aside. In a clean, dry

continued

mixing bowl, whip the egg whites to the soft peak stage. They should look thick and foamy and start to turn white. Slowly add the remaining 1/4 cup of sugar and whip on high speed until firm peaks hold. Gently fold into the passion fruit curd in 3 additions, each after the previous one is about 90 percent incorporated.

Spoon the filling into the cooled crust and chill at least 3 hours. If you freeze the pie overnight, it becomes easier to cut into wedges. You can even serve it frozen for a refreshing summertime treat. If you prefer to serve it soft, refrigerate the slices of pie after they have been cut and they will slowly thaw out.

To make the coulis, place all of the ingredients in a saucepan and bring to a boil. Simmer over medium-high heat, stirring constantly, until most of the liquid has evaporated, about 5 minutes. Let cool. If you desire a smoother texture, puree in a food processor or strain out the seeds.

Spoon a tablespoon of coulis across a dessert plate and place a slice of pie on top.

TIRAMISU

{INTERMEDIATE}   Makes 8 generous portions

Tiramisu literally translates to "pick-me-up," and *this* is the recipe that reminds me of when my husband proposed to me. In Italy. At sunset. At a castle-turned-outdoor-restaurant on a cliff 200 feet above the Mediterranean Sea. I honestly can't remember if we ordered dessert that night. We were too high on our new engagement. But every time I bite into the cool creaminess of tiramisu, I am transported to that evening in Italy and how excited we both were. It was truly our own little Italian "pick-me-up."

LADYFINGER SPONGE

2 egg whites

$1/2$ cup / 113 g sugar

$1/4$ teaspoon / 1.3 g vanilla extract

2 egg yolks

$1/4$ cup / 31 g tapioca starch

$1/4$ cup / 47 g potato starch

$1/4$ cup / 40 g sweet white rice flour

Pinch / .5 g salt

$1/4$ cup / 36 g confectioners' sugar

ESPRESSO SYRUP

1 cup / 227 ml strong espresso, cooled, or 5 tablespoons / 25 g instant coffee dissolved in 1 cup / 227 ml water

$1/2$ cup / 113 g sugar

MASCARPONE CREAM

3 egg whites

$3/4$ cup / 170 g sugar

3 egg yolks

$1^1/3$ cups / 312 g mascarpone cheese

$1/4$ cup / 57 g silver rum

Pinch / .5 g salt

$1/2$ cup / 59 g heavy cream, very cold

Sifted cocoa powder, for garnish

Preheat the oven to 300°F. Using a pencil or pen, draw twenty-four 3-inch circles on two sheets of parchment paper, leaving about $1^1/2$ inches between each circle. Line two baking pans with the paper, pencil side down, and set aside.

To make the ladyfinger sponge, in a clean, dry mixing bowl, whip the egg whites on medium-high speed until thick and foamy. Slowly add $1/4$ cup of the sugar and the vanilla on medium speed and whip until glossy and thick and medium peaks form, about 3 minutes. Transfer the meringue to a clean, dry bowl. In the first mixing bowl, whip the egg yolks and the remaining $1/4$ cup of sugar on high speed for about 6 minutes, until thick, fluffy, and tripled in volume and the mixture reaches the "ribbon stage": if you drip a spoonful of the mixture across the surface, it forms a ribbon visible for 3 seconds before it sinks back into the mixture. Sprinkle the starches over the yolk mixture and fold in. Add the rice flour and salt and fold in as well. Then very gently fold the meringue into the yolk mixture in 3 additions, each after the previous one is about 90 percent incorporated.

Spoon the batter into a pastry bag or gallon-sized ziplock bag with a corner snipped off and, using the drawn circles as a guide, pipe the batter into 3-inch circles on the parchment paper. Sift confectioners' sugar over the top of each circle and bake until lightly golden and set, 15 to 20 minutes.

To make the espresso syrup, stir together the espresso and sugar and boil just until the sugar dissolves. Set aside to cool.

continued

To make the mascarpone cream, in a clean, dry bowl, whip the egg whites to the soft peak stage and add $1/4$ cup of the sugar. Whip on high speed until medium-stiff peaks hold, 4 to 5 minutes. Transfer the meringue to a clean, dry bowl. In the first mixing bowl, whip the egg yolks and the remaining $1/2$ cup of sugar on high speed until light, fluffy, and tripled in volume and the mixture reaches the ribbon stage (see page 119), about 6 minutes. Add the mascarpone, rum, and salt to the yolk mixture and whip on low speed until well combined. Gently fold the meringue into the mascarpone mixture in 3 additions, each after the previous one is about 90 percent incorporated. Then whip the heavy cream to medium-stiff peaks and fold into the mascarpone mixture using the same process, in 3 additions.

To assemble, set out eight 8-ounce juice glasses that are $3 1/2$ inches in diameter. Soak a circle of the ladyfinger sponge in the espresso syrup and place at the bottom of each glass. Top with a dollop of the mascarpone cream. Repeat twice more and dust the top of each tiramisu with a little bit of the cocoa powder. Eat with a long-handled dessert spoon.